Blessings
Through the Seasons

VICKIE PAPPAS

D1567724

Phileo Blessings
Jacksonville, FL

Book and cover design by Sagaponack Books & Design
Cover painting by Brad Scott

Scripture is from the English Standard Version (ESV) Bible
unless otherwise noted.

ISBNs:
978-1-7377496-3-9 (softcover)
978-1-7377496-4-6 (hardcover)
978-1-7377496-5-3 (e-book)

Library of Congress Control Number: 2023923621

Summary: A Christian devotional based on Bible verses,
with personal reflections to inspire and uplift as you go
through the seasons.

REL036000 Religion / Inspirational
REL012020 Religion / Christian Living / Devotional
REL012120 Religion / Christian Living / Spiritual Growth
REL012070 Religion / Christian Living / Personal Growth

Phileo Blessings
Jacksonville, Florida

Printed and bound in the United States of America
First Edition

In loving memory of my parents, Bill and Della, who inspired me to have faith in God and look for the blessings in every circumstance; and for all in need of comfort, hope, or peace to trust the Lord is with you through every season of the year and every season of your life.

Contents

FOREWORD

As Vickie's pastor for the last fifteen years, I have had the honor to see Vickie Pappas's genuine walk of faith through the different seasons she has encountered. When we first met, I saw a lovely, vivacious woman who always looked perfect on the surface. Then, through the tragic and untimely death of a young student who had put her faith in Jesus through the church which I had the privilege of serving, I came to realize the love Vickie finds in Jesus runs deep and is unshakeable. She radiates a genuine faith rooted in her commitment to the Creator.

In her first book, *Blessings Along the Way*, Vickie compiled weekly devotionals that started as inspiring texts she sent to others in her personal ministry. With the encouragement of those who received them, she put a sampling of them into a book. She used her own experiences, divine encounters, and Scripture, which I believe come straight from the heart of God to speak life to others—including me.

Vickie recognizes that we all go through experiences and seasons of life that we can understand more fully by seeking our Savior and the abundant life He has for us in Him. In this latest book of devotionals, *Blessings Through the Seasons*, Vickie again uses Scriptures and personal stories as she compares the seasons in nature to the seasons in life—always with joy, always with the understanding that God has plans for us that will get us through.

No matter what you are experiencing, in this book you will find something that reaches into your heart, gives you hope, lifts you up, and lets you know that the Creator is with you and loves you through every season of your life.

Joby Martin, Lead Pastor
The Church of Eleven22

INTRODUCTION

As long as the Earth endures, seedtime and harvest, cold and heat, summer and winter, day and night never cease.
Genesis 8:22

In the book of Genesis we have evidence which shows seasons have been here since the beginning of time. Everything God designs is for a purpose, including the seasons of our lives. We can allow each season to draw us closer to Christ so we may grow and be fruitful in this life and for His Kingdom.

We walk through spiritual seasons in life similar to those in nature. Be mindful when entering new seasons: transition can be the most vulnerable place of insecurity. At the same time, it is the most significant place of opportunity. While God may have led us away from a place of comfort, He has a purpose for where He has placed us now. The beginning of each new season presents the perfect opportunity to start fresh in different areas of our lives. Whether this new season has presented us with blessings, challenges, or both, we can find comfort that God promises to be with us every step of the way.

In *Blessings Through the Seasons*, I relate the seasons of life to the seasons in nature. How seamlessly our Heavenly Father has weaved together four seasons in creation.

Spring is certainly a time of beauty and new growth. It's when new seeds are planted and regrowth of brightly colored perennials occurs. Springtime also corresponds to a season of spiritual renewal and refreshment in our lives.

Summer brings warmth and sunshine along with heat and thunderstorms. We might be optimistic, carefree, and peaceful, or flooded, frightened, and restless. We must keep in mind that God brings sunshine or rain when He wills it.

Fall ushers in colors and coolness, along with tangible and intangible things which need to be falling away. The days get shorter and leaves assume breathtaking vibrant hues. It's the season of harvest and thanksgiving, shedding, and change. We also can experience seasons of transition when we recognize that we are changing.

In winter we see and feel more darkness and isolation. The days become even shorter and temperatures drop, but God might be calling us to a season of restful peace and shedding a layer so that we, too, can draw nearer to Him.

May the God of hope fill you with all
joy and peace as you trust in Him, so
that you may overflow with hope by the
power of the Holy Spirit.

—Romans 15:13

Spring

Calm

I have calmed and quieted my soul. Psalm 131

*H*ow do you quiet your soul? The Hebrew word *calmed* translated in this verse literally means "to make level."

In the middle of our busy lives, we can be like King David and let God level and calm our soul. King David repeatedly writes in the Psalms that God is what calms him. We often say he was a man after God's own heart, and that is what he sought. When David's anxiety threatened to undo him, David turned to the one who was able to meet him in his soul and provide comfort.

Staying calm allows us to think logically and make wise decisions accordingly. Clarity of mind is important when dealing with any problem. In a world of chaos, a calm mind is extremely important. So how do we attain it? Breathing deeply is a great way to calm our spirit. In the Book of Psalms, the psalmists literally pause to invite us to take a breath with Him, breathing in God's love and mercy and breathing out our worries. Breathing deeply in times of worry is a calm way to slow down and be in God's presence. I have found peace in breath prayers. I inhale Scripture quotes with God's promises such as "Come, Holy Spirit" … and exhale "Fill my heart." Breathing prayers are a beautiful way to oxygenate our soul with God's peace and to restore calm.

In relationship with God we discover rest and ease, which revolves around simply being with Him. In that space we find a calm and quiet soul.

How do you calm your mind and quiet your soul?

Praise Him

Let everything that has breath praise the Lord. Praise the Lord.
Psalm 150:6

Yesterday in church we sang, "Praise God, from whom all blessings flow. Praise Him, all creatures here below. Praise Him, above ye Heavenly Host. Praise Father, Son, and Holy Ghost!"

Beautiful and simple, these twenty-five words are known around the world as "the Doxology." One of the most widely known hymns of all time, it was written in 1674 by Thomas Ken, for his students at Winchester College at Oxford University, to sing upon arising in the morning and at bedtime each night. At its core, the Doxology is both a hymn of praise and thanksgiving, and a good reminder that God is most glorified in our heartfelt expression of praise.

I remember, as a young girl, sitting beside Grandmother Mellie—known as Mamaw Mellie—at Dante Methodist Church in Knoxville, Tennessee, and singing this while holding her hand. On the surface, these lyrics seem modest and memorable. Reflecting on her own life, she would remind me that simple doesn't mean shallow. Plain does not exclude profound. God is glorified in our heartfelt expression of praise. My grandmother appeared on the outside to be a simple and plain country woman, but her wisdom and deep-rooted faith penetrated everyone she encountered—especially me. It's not by chance she was born on Christmas Day. I'm forever grateful she encouraged me to "Praise God, from whom all blessings flow."

Do you have a Mamaw in your life, or can you be a Mamaw to someone else?

Pruning

I am the vine; you are the branches. If you remain in me and I in you, you will bear much fruit; apart from me you can do nothing. John 15:5

I read a garden sign recently: YOUR MIND IS A GARDEN, YOUR THOUGHTS ARE THE SEEDS; YOU CAN GROW FLOWERS, OR YOU CAN GROW WEEDS. Growing flowers instead of weeds in the garden of our hearts and minds is like staying connected to God—like a branch is attached to its vine and depends on it for life.

I did some pruning in my yard, preparing the rose bushes for spring. Clipped back, they temporarily look barren; however, removing dead branches will allow for new growth and beautiful blooms. God's primary concern for pruning off the old is the same for us. Spiritual pruning enhances personal growth. We need to allow the "gardener" to prune us of our negative behaviors, choices, and deeds so we can grow on the inside and be a light for others.

I have found it helpful to evaluate my life and choices periodically and ask God to show me if there are things that need pruning. Although pruning can be painful, it is miserable to drag around dead branches—old wounds, negative attitudes, and unhealthy relationships from the past that keep us from moving forward, enjoying life to the fullest, and honoring Him. Even though we may feel uncomfortable, the best thing we can do is allow God to reveal what needs to be pruned, and watch how abundant the fruit will be.

How does your garden grow?

Hero

May the God of hope fill you with all joy and peace as you trust in him, so that you may overflow with hope by the power of the Holy Spirit. Romans 15:13

We hear the word *hero* tossed around a lot. I read a book, *Hope Unseen*, by Captain Scotty Smiley with Doug Crandall. In my opinion, Smiley is no doubt an American hero. In 2005 he was leading his platoon in the Iraq War, when a suicide car-bomb detonated right in front of him. The blast sent shrapnel through the air and into his eyes, leaving him blind and temporarily paralyzed.

He went through a long stretch of healing, and slowly God showed Smiley that the current plan was far better than the plan he'd had for himself. Smiley refused to allow his disability to prevent him from serving his country and others. Once he was declared mentally and physically fit, he returned to service and became the first blind active-duty officer in military history. He became a triathlete, surfed in Hawaii, skied in Colorado, skydived in Texas, and climbed Mount Rainier in Washington. He also earned his MBA and taught at West Point.

He says his faith allowed him to be the man he is today. God gave him strength through despair and the hope to persevere. Smiley chooses to look at what God has given him: his ability with which he can glorify and praise the Lord. Though he can no longer physically see, he says he looks at life and anyone else through the eyes of love and the lens of God.

Where in your life is there hope unseen?

Waiting

Truly, my soul waiteth upon God: from him cometh my salvation. He only is my rock and my salvation, He is my defence; I shall not be greatly moved. Psalm 62:1-2 (KJV)

We often find ourselves waiting for something. It can be something as simple as the light to turn green, our turn at the checkout counter, or the cake to bake, or it can be as difficult as waiting for a baby to arrive, a health diagnosis, or the results of a job interview. Waiting is part of life. The question is: How do we wait?

Waiting gives us the opportunity to draw our hearts closer to God. Waiting time is never a wasted season. Change is a process. Waiting seasons are found all through Scripture. Joseph heard from God in a dream that there was a waiting season. Noah heard from God and waited. … Then the rains came. In anticipation of God's future plans for us, we are more alert to God's voice when we are waiting to hear from Him. Our eyes are also quicker to see and recognize His power and provisions in times of waiting.

Many times we experience a pause, but like a comma in a sentence, it's not the end; it's only a time to wait. Waiting gets our attention. As in nature, between seedtime and harvest comes a time of waiting; the same is true for us. After we plant seeds of honor and trust, we feel like nothing may be happening. Yet God is working behind the scenes, and eventually our seeds of patience break through like a seed pushes through the soil and becomes something beautiful! Trusting in God assures us all things are worth the wait.

How do you wait?

Stretch

And he looked around at them with anger, grieved at their hardness of heart, and said to the man, "Stretch out your hand." He stretched it out, and his hand was restored. Mark 3:5

There are many examples of stretching in the Bible. In Mark 3:5, we see that stretching comes before the blessing of the man with the withered hand being restored. It was the Sabbath and working was forbidden on that day. Jesus told the man to stand and stretch out his hand. He said, *My Father never stops working, and so I work too. (John 5:17)* In Exodus 14:26-27, God told Moses to stretch out his rod over the Red Sea. Moses obeyed, and God stretched out His hands and parted the Red Sea.

We all hear about the importance of stretching. Daily stretching helps loosen and strengthen our muscles. Like stretching our body, stretching our faith is also a daily practice which strengthens our spiritual muscles and our connection to Christ.

How do we stretch when we feel tightened by worry, fear, or anxiety? Simply by putting our confidence in the Lord. In His way and His timing, He will come through. Jeremiah 29:11-12 (NIV) says: *"For I know the plans I have for you," declares the Lord, "plans to prosper you and not to harm you, plans to give you hope and a future. Then you will call on me and come and pray to me and I will listen to you."* Surrendering things we can't control by stretching out our hands, knowing the Lord will be faithful to deliver, brings us great comfort.

What can you stretch out and release to the hands of the Lord?

Servant

His master replied, "Well done, good and faithful servant!"
Matthew 25:23 (NIV)

This verse was the common denominator at my dad's funeral service on January 30, 2023. At eighty-nine years old, William Easterday lived his life through faith, given to him by grace. He humbly lived for God and God's glory, not for his own. It was so beautiful to witness both young and old come together in attendance; they shared stories of the way my dad had inspired and influenced their lives. Many of the heartfelt actions they recounted were unknown to me since my dad was such a modest man.

While I was growing up, each week an eighteen-year-old named Tommy came to our home. He could not read, yet was promoted each year to the next grade in a school system which he learned to outsmart and manipulate. He relied on others because he was too embarrassed to admit he could not read. Many nights, Tommy had dinner with our family. My mom embraced loving and serving him as well. My brother, Billy, and I had a beautiful front-row seat to true servanthood and warm hospitality. Though we were only ten and thirteen, we watched our dad promote integrity, build confidence, and influence this young man.

My dad made a real and lasting impression on Tommy's life, and ours too. Tommy's goal was to be able to find and read both his name and my dad's name in the phone book. I can still remember him calling to thank my dad and saying he did it!—Mr. William Easterday, at 1513 Dalewood Drive, 904-724-3132. That was one great moment for us all.

How can you serve God and others?

Influence

Let no one despise you for your youth, but set the believers an example in speech, in conduct, in love, in faith, in purity. 1 Timothy 4:12

I can still remember, as a young girl, a specific mentor and role model who lovingly influenced me. Her name was Betty Workman. She worked at the church across the street from my house and was my vacation Bible school teacher for years. Betty inspired me to dream big, pray daily, and trust God in all things.

I was in the fifth grade and a patrol girl. I wanted to run for captain of the patrols. A girl had never been selected, yet Betty encouraged me to run and helped me write my speech. In my pigtails, I stood and delivered my speech. Looking up in the auditorium I saw sweet Betty standing in the back, smiling. Much to my surprise I was chosen by my fellow student patrols to be their captain. After a big hug, the first thing Betty did was take my hands and pray. She thanked God for granting me the opportunity to make a difference at my school. Years later Betty ended up with ALS, still smiling and inspiring me through voice activation, even in the midst of such a dreadful disease.

When we look at the life and teachings of Jesus, no one would deny that Jesus had the most positive impact on human history. His approach was not manipulative or self-serving. He led by example and by serving others.

Betty served Christ and was a light to many. I gave her my captain patrol badge on my last visit before she passed away. Her belief in me was a big reason I had the courage to run.

Who can you inspire?

Awakening

The heavens declare the glory of God, and the sky above pro-claims his handiwork. Psalm 19:1

A primary way God nourishes our souls with His loving presence is through the beauty of nature. Have you ever experienced a profound sense of wonder while enjoying the outdoors? So many things in nature give us pause and astound us.

This happened to me on a beautiful spring day while on the west coast of Florida, surrounded by turquoise water, blue skies, blooming flowers, and palm trees. I paused and prayed as I took a screen shot in my mind of such glory. A stranger happened to pass by with the word "Wow" on the back of his shirt. As I looked at the beauty surrounding me, I too thought "Wow." When we see a sunrise or sunset, remember God gave us light and warmth and hope. Psalm 113:3 reminds us: *From the rising of the sun to its setting, the name of the Lord is to be praised!* I believe that in taking the time to pause, letting the beauty and mystery of all God's creation into our consciousness, awakens us with an even deeper longing to know our Heavenly Father.

Nature reveals to us God's beauty, glory, power, presence, and, most of all, His loving care. This week let's allow our hearts to be stirred as we discover God's unwavering desire to speak to us through the beauty of His creation. Prepare for surprises—life's most treasured moments usually come unannounced.

What does God's handiwork in nature reveal to you?

Encouragement

When he arrived and witnessed the grace of God, he rejoiced and began to encourage them all with resolute heart to remain true to the Lord. Acts 11:23

Are you in need of encouragement? At some point we all feel pressure and stress, and we are in need of support. In the Bible, Barnabas was a man of encouragement; his name means "son of encouragement." This spotlights his empathy and aptitude for offering hope and consolation to others in times of affliction and doubt.

Barnabas was also sincere and generous. He sold his land and gave the profits to the apostles, knowing his contribution would be distributed to anyone in need. Knowing God's love and walking in a relationship with Him is the greatest encouragement we could ever receive, no matter how big the storm.

I believe the circle we surround ourselves with is of great importance as well. Think about your circle of friends. Who encourages you? Take time to fill your heart and space with these kinds of friendships. Sitting across from Robin, a childhood friend who now lives in London, I listened as she shared her wisdom and authentic encouragement about this book and the following of my dreams. She is a brilliant, successful, and generous woman with a huge heart of compassion that inspires others to reach their full potential. I left feeling empowered, knowing I can do all things through Christ Who gives me strength. I'm also grateful for deeply rooted childhood friends like Robin, who are willing to pour authentic encouragement into my soul.

Think about who is in your circle. Do they speak life and encouragement?

Bloom

The righteous will flourish like a palm tree, they will grow like a cedar of Lebanon, planted in the House of the Lord, they will flourish in the courts of God. Psalm 92:12-13

We've all heard the phrase, "to bloom where we are planted." The word *bloom*, which is a verb, implies that we have to be intentional. Blooming means "to produce something beautiful." When something is planted, it is placed there intentionally. This is a reminder that where we are right now is where God placed us. While writing *Blessings Through the Seasons*, I was reflecting on the places and circumstances where God has planted me. How appropriate God's timing is. I happened to be sitting surrounded by beautiful flowers in a lovely café named "Bloom."

When we submit our lives to Christ, He prepares us and grows us. He is always there through the process to guide, water, correct, and encourage. Though good or bad circumstances may have brought us to this spot, God has prepared the soil for us to bloom where we are. Sometimes during the pressure of difficult seasons, God is sifting us free of negative debris. After the sifting, all that remains is the goodness of God. He allows us to grow and lean on Him.

A caterpillar turns into a butterfly after the struggle of breaking free from its cocoon. Pearls are created when a clam is irritated by a grain of sand, forests regrow and thrive after a forest fire. Just as in nature, growth, change, and flourishing go hand in hand with difficult seasons and fiery trials. To bloom and thrive where we are planted means to develop deep roots reflecting the goodness of God.

How can you flourish and bloom where you are planted now?

Honesty

Honesty guides good people; dishonesty destroys treacherous people. Proverbs 11:3

Honesty is more than the words we say. It's a posture of the heart. Think about honesty. What is the first thing that comes to mind?

In 2008 *New York Magazine* ran a comprehensive article about research concerning kids and lying. Researchers taught the story of George Washington and the cherry tree. In the story, George goes to his father and confesses that he cut down the tree. His father replies, "Hearing you tell the truth instead of a lie is better than if I had 1,000 cherry trees." Researchers found the story of George Washington reduced lying by 43 percent. When children learned the worth of honesty as they did in the story of George Washington, they seemed to want to tell the truth.

Why is honesty so important? We've all heard "Honesty is the best policy." We've had this statement ingrained in us as children. Honesty is spoken about throughout Scripture. The Old and New Testament authors write about the importance of being honest with others because it maintains trust and unity. When we are honest, we build strength of character that will allow us to be of great service to God and others. When we choose honesty, we are known to be trustworthy. We are blessed with peace of mind and self-respect, as well as being trusted by others. Learning to express honesty tucked in an envelope of kindness can be one of the greatest areas of growth in our lives. Ultimately, it propels us into deeper and more authentic relationships.

Is honesty your best policy?

Zeal

Never be lacking in zeal, but keep your spiritual fervor, serving the Lord. Romans 12:11

Zeal is defined as "great energy or enthusiasm in pursuit of a cause or an objective." While at HarborChase senior facility in Jasper, Alabama, I met Miss Lenear Stewart Jones. At ninety-eight years old, she's still full of zeal for Jesus and has a zest for life. I sat and listened as she told about her walk with the Lord. She was converted at the age of thirteen, in an old-fashioned tent revival complete with sawdust on the floor. She managed not only to get her alcoholic father to go with her, but during the revival she also got him to the altar. He was saved that night as well, laying his flask of alcohol on the altar. The pastor leading the revival was so overwhelmed about what he had witnessed that he shared it the next morning on his radio program, saying, "A little child shall lead them."

Though it might appear life can be routine, Lenear still finds a way to shake things up. She loves her HarborChase family, and enjoys reading, singing, attending Bible study, Sunday school, cooking classes, and praying with her fellow residents. With her hair done and lipstick on, she said her life testimony is that she has been transformed by God's grace, chooses to be obedient to His Word, is passionate in pursuit of His love, and shares that love with all those she encounters.

In 2014 she slipped outside and broke her hip. While lying in the snow for more than two hours she prayed, knowing and trusting God would somehow rescue her. He did, and she still has zeal to share. I left HarborChase with a heart full of zeal from Miss Lenear Stewart Jones.

Possibility

Jesus looked at them and said, "With man this is impossible, but with God all things are possible." Matthew 19:26

Possibility is powerful. God promises that with Him all things are possible. Possibility means we are not limited. The door of possibilities is in front of us. The question is: Will we walk through it?

How do we walk through it? By placing our faith in God and trusting that He is at work for our benefit—even when we can't see it. God is a miracle worker and the God of possibility. This concept is the basis of a book by bestselling author Pastor Joby Martin with *New York Times* bestselling author Charles Martin. *Anything Is Possible: How Nine Miracles of Jesus Reveal God's Love for You* is an insightful and spiritually rich look at the miracles of Christ. The pastor examines the Bible and tells readers that God still performs miracles today. The book reveals something unique: how God wants to teach us about the miraculous power available to every believer. Pastor Martin reminds us not to seek miracles themselves, but the one who performs them.

In many other Bible stories, God provided and proved His power over seemingly impossible situations: Daniel surviving being thrown into the lions' den, Noah building his ark on dry land, and the parting of the Red Sea while Moses held out his staff. When we choose to trust, choose to walk by faith, choose to look for His goodness, we are assured that with God all things are possible.

What impossibilities do you need to surrender to God?

Freedom

Greater love has no one than this, that someone lay down his life for his friends. John 15:13

Memorial Day is about remembering. It has "memory" in it. Remembering stirs within me a sense of gratitude and appreciation for those who fought and died for our freedom. For many, it's the kickoff of summer activities and is met by proudly flying our American flag. Originally it was a day to decorate the graves of soldiers, and it later became a day to remember their service.

I read about Arlington National Cemetery's Flags-In. Small flags are placed exactly one boot length in front of more than 260,000 headstones. This tradition has taken place every Memorial Day since the 3rd US Infantry Regiment (The Old Guard) was designated as the army's official ceremonial unit in 1948. It serves as a reminder for those who made the ultimate sacrifice—laying down their life for our freedom—and creates a sea of patriotism and a united atmosphere for all who visit their loved ones to pay tribute to our nation's heroes.

Inspired by this, I strengthened my resolve to show honor for those who served God, my country, and others. I purchased small flags to line my driveway, in reverence and to pay tribute to those brave soldiers who were willing to give up their life for our freedom.

This Memorial Day, will you join me and pause in prayer out of respect and gratitude for all those who have given up their lives for our freedom? May the example of their sacrifice inspire in us the selfless love of Jesus Christ.

Freedom is a beautiful gift. I encourage you to pause and remember.

Listening

A wise man will hear and increase in learning, and a man of understanding will acquire wise counsel. Proverbs 1:5

Every day we have countless voices telling us what to do, what to buy, and how to live. We live in a world with so many platforms to voice thoughts and opinions, but who are we listening to?

The human ear is exposed to between 20,000 and 30,000 words a day. We may not be able to control everything we hear, but we do get to decide what or who we listen to, which will affect our lives and the lives of those around us.

The word *listen* appears 278 times in the Bible. The word *Shema* in the Hebrew Bible is translated as "listen," but it means far more than just to listen. It means to really pay attention. How often have you heard someone say "Are you listening to me?" Have we lost the ability to actively listen? Active listening requires disciplined silence during which we strive to understand the thoughts, feelings, and meaning behind words. Good listening is a means of grace and it develops deeper relationships and understanding.

Choosing to listen to God's voice over others requires us to humble ourselves. Through quiet time in prayer, we can hear His voice, which leads us to make choices that pursue holiness and result in peace. He directs our steps and accompanies us on a steady journey, even when circumstances don't seem to make sense.

As we are reminded in James 1:19: *Know this, my beloved brothers: let every person be quick to hear, slow to speak, slow to anger.*

Do you practice active listening?

Smile

A glad heart makes a cheerful face, but by sorrow of the heart the spirit is crushed. Proverbs 15:13

When I was entering the supermarket, a stranger passing me going out greeted me with a big smile. I smiled back and was inspired to continue smiling at others. Walking through the produce section, I reflected on the wonderful warm feeling a simple smile can bring.

The effect of a smile is powerful. Nothing warms the temperature of a relationship like a smile which comes from the heart. Everybody knows the expression one wears on their face is far more important than the clothes they wear on their back. A smile costs nothing, yet creates much. It's the best way to give daylight to the discouraged, sunshine to the sad, and it is certainly nature's best antidote for any kind of trouble. An insincere grin doesn't fool anybody—it's mechanical; however, a real heartwarming smile glows from within.

Physicians say it takes fewer muscles to smile than to frown. More than that, a smile can be a reflection of the joy in our heart, regardless of our circumstances. A smile is like an emotional handshake which draws people together. That's because we associate smiling with feeling positive. When you generally care about others, they can pick it up through your smile—it can't be contrived because others see when it's not genuine. Trends in fashion may come and go, but smiles are always in style. A smile brings a ray of sunshine into any day.

Who's in need of your warm smile?

Unexpected

The heart of man plans his way, but the Lord establishes his steps. Proverbs 16:9

After reading this Scripture, I pondered about being open to the unexpected. We may write things on our calendar, but are we truly open to change when things don't go the way we expected? While our planning is important, God is the author of our life story.

Ecclesiastes is written by King Solomon, known for his wisdom. He discusses the ebb and flow of life: in chapter 3 he focuses on the concept of time in the heart of a man; in verse 11 he explains that God is the holder of time and He makes everything beautiful in its time. Solomon reveals the ups and downs of life as normal, and urges us to choose an eternal perspective even if we don't have all the answers.

I have read the book, *The Gift of the Unexpected: Discovering Who You Were Meant to Be When Life Goes Off Plan*, by Jillian Benfield. She was a TV news anchor/reporter and had high hopes and expectations of what her life would be. Then her life took an unexpected turn when she started her family. One child needed open heart surgery, her third child was diagnosed with a rare health issue, Jillian suffered a miscarriage, and she has a son born with Down's syndrome. Through all of this she has become an advocate for children with disabilities and has witnessed firsthand the gifts tucked into the unexpected. She now travels around the country inspiring others to find purpose and sharing how God uses our unexpected circumstances and turns them for good. He gives us the liberty to decide how we will move forward.

How do you respond to the unexpected?

Unity

How good and pleasant it is when God's people live together in unity. Psalm 133:1

In our fractured culture, we are surrounded by tension and strife. Hate, dissension, and contempt flood our news feeds daily. This creates anxiety and division. The Bible instructs us to keep the unity of the spirit in the bond of peace.

I will always remember the flowers and sign, DON'T DENY—UNIFY, outside Emanuel AME Church in Charleston, South Carolina, after the 2015 tragic shooting there. Then, seeing thousands of people form a "Bridge to Peace" unity chain on the Arthur Ravenel Jr. Bridge, praying and joining hands to unite in strength against division and hate. When God's people come together in unity to achieve a common goal, their aligned effort brings divine power and transforming effects to the world, and serves to remind us: Where there is unity, there is strength.

Our unity isn't based on shared cultures, personal interests, or opinions, but on something more profound. It's not what we have in common that matters, but who we have in common. We don't have to see eye to eye to walk hand in hand. Jesus taught His disciples that their unity was essential to their effectiveness.

John 13:35 (NIV) says: *By this everyone will know that you are my disciples, if you love one another.* May God use us to be bridge builders in a hurting world which desperately needs to see the Gospel lived out each day.

Do you show the spirit of unity?

Cherish

The one who gets wisdom loves life, the one who cherishes understanding will soon prosper. Proverbs 19:8 (NIV)

Cherish. What does that word mean to you? According to the dictionary, cherish has three methods of action: "protect and care for lovingly, hold dearly, and keep in one's mind." Many things are attached to the word *cherish*, but will they last? Instead of cherishing the temporary, why not look at cherishing people and opportunities God has placed in our life, and cherish them and our connection with our Lord even more. God gives us His unconditional love and His open arms. Cherish not only the moments of blessings, but also the molding, pruning, and refining He does in our lives, even through difficult seasons. Doing so will help us grow closer to Him.

The writers of the Old Testament urge us to value and cherish wisdom and understanding from God's perspective. The lessons, hardships, challenges, and celebrations of today are the moments to be present for and cherish. Things cherished are precious treasures to be cared for delicately.

I'm cherishing our annual girls' trip here at Clear Lake in Indiana. Sitting outside by the lake on a peaceful morning, watching the sunrise, my soul was filled. To recognize and cherish moments as they happen will help us feel thankful and will foster a more positive outlook. I don't want to rush through life and miss special moments. It feels like we've almost stepped back in time when we reunite and share our many years and fun stories of friendship, nurturing, and love. Most importantly, we are cherishing one another.

What do you cherish?

Temptation

So when the woman saw that the tree was good for food, and that it was a delight to the eyes, and that the tree was desired to make one wise, she took of its fruit and ate, and she also gave some to her husband who was with her, and he ate. Genesis 3:6

Our world surrounds us with temptation. It is everywhere, and if we are not careful it can easily slip in. For example, I have celiac disease and one dose of gluten is toxic to my body. I've found that even fancy restaurants can have camouflaged gluten, which may be used as a binding agent in delicious soups and sauces. However, after only a few bites I know I'm in big trouble. Sometimes the server may not understand my inquiry and how serious it is for me, and doesn't check with the chef. This happened recently and I struggled through the aftereffects. It's just not worth the temptation of a piece of chocolate cake or a slice of warm homemade bread— something tempting which looks and smells delicious but is harmful to my body.

The incident brought to mind how the same is true with our personal temptations, which dishonor God, and how easily even spiritual allergies can slip up on us and be destructive. They can be deceptive—seeming so small— and sometimes we're not aware of the unpleasant side effects until it's too late. A good example is Eve, when she was lured by Satan to eat the forbidden fruit. Because Eve yielded to temptation and shared the fruit with Adam, who also knew it was forbidden, they were banished from the Garden of Eden and our struggle with sin began.

What do you do when temptation creeps in?

Touch

Moved with compassion, Jesus touched their eyes; and immediately they regained their sight and followed Him. Matthew 20:34

Jesus gained a reputation for reaching out and touching people. He went about healing and restoring the afflicted simply by touching them. He touched the eyes of blind people, and they could see. He healed and cleansed the leper. When He touched Peter's mother-in-law, her fever left her body. He comforted John by placing His right hand on him, saying, "Do not be afraid." What a calming touch Jesus provided.

According to the American Medical Association, "Touch can reduce heart rate and blood pressure and help us to feel calmer. Touch reduces the release of cortisol and seems to have a beneficial role in our immune response. Touch can strongly transmit a sense of being accepted and cared for and can reduce a sense of loneliness."

God gives us opportunities to extend His grace and compassion with a gentle touch. I experienced this recently with Nancy, a sweet eighty-nine-year-old lady I met at a country church. When we shook hands, she asked me not to let go of her hand. She lives alone and shared how much comfort she felt by the touch of simply holding hands. I felt the same peace and comfort. I looked up at the wall behind her and saw footprints and these words: "Where have you seen God's footprints this week?" I realized I just did, in meeting Nancy.

Who can you comfort with the simple and kind touch of your hands?

Good News

Since my youth, God, you have taught me, and to this day I declare your marvelous deeds. Psalm 71:17 (NIV)

One day my dad stopped over and, while sharing the good news about the bass he had caught in my neighborhood pond, he referenced an inspiring sermon from Pastor Jerry Sweat, about spreading or sharing good news. Pastor Jerry's sermon was about a young friend who persisted in sharing the Good News of the Gospel with him while in middle school. The friend continued inviting him to church, and when Jerry accepted the invitation to church and asked Jesus into his heart, his life was changed—resulting in a career in ministry and sharing God's light and love with others.

We all get excited about sharing news about a new baby, an exciting basketball game, or a new restaurant, but sometimes we are hesitant to share the best news of all: the Good News of the Gospel. As we approach Easter and the resurrection of our Lord, there is no better time to share the story of God's gift of salvation through the death, burial, and resurrection of Jesus.

What an honor to be able to share the story of God's grace and mercy that has been revealed to us in the Bible! As we draw closer to our Heavenly Father, the more His light and joy will shine from within us. We may never know the difference it can make in someone else's life.

Who can you share the Good News of the Gospel with?

Protection

He who dwells in the shelter of the Most High will abide in the shadow of the Almighty. Psalm 91:1

Someone recently pointed out, "It's interesting that the world must have gotten its distress 911 number from God's answer to our distress call, Psalm 91:1." That is what Psalm 91 is all about: shelter. Our Heavenly Father has a secret place in His arms which protects us from the storms raging in the world around us.

During a difficult season, Psalm 91:1 was the Scripture I read daily. The number to call in an emergency is 911. It is who we call when we are in trouble or see it. Psalm 91:1 reminds us Who to call on when we have a problem. This verse has been classically known as God's telephone number. Trouble comes in all forms. Like we need medical insurance for our physical health when there is an emergency, we also need spiritual insurance coverage—which only Christ can give for spiritual emergencies.

While out for a walk, I noticed my neighbor who had just fallen outside and hit her head. I immediately called 911 and sat with her, holding her and praying out this Psalm until the EMTs arrived. Thank goodness for 911 in this crisis and their immediate assistance. Also for the ability to call out in faith requesting help from God. My neighbor is now fine after a visit to the hospital and the proper medical attention. She was so grateful for the EMTs' professionalism and for the prayer over her too. She felt calm and comforted even in the midst of this crisis.

To abide in the shadow of the Almighty, we must first choose to dwell in the shelter of the Most High.

Moving Forward

The LORD replied, "My Presence will go with you, and I will give you rest." Exodus 33:14 (NIV)

Choosing to view moving into a new home as a crosswalk to new prospects full of blessings, possibilities, and fruitfulness from God is very helpful. Remember, with endings come new beginnings.

Helping my friend box up, discard, and donate her household items as she prepares for a move, we celebrated the new season God has in store for her. We prayed together over her new home as the moving process began, with confidence that God is leading and protecting her. It brought much comfort. We talked about the tendency to pack everything into boxes and keep it all. Likewise, we have a tendency to take our requests, problems, and struggles, handing them to God, but then pick them up again and carry them with us. Why do we hang on to things we know we should release?

Some boxes I moved years ago went straight to the attic and have never been opened again. It's human nature to cling to what is comfortable. Sometimes, in order to seek God we must get rid of the unnecessary boxes. As we learn from the Bible, in transition we can become transformed. Prayer is a wonderful way to ask God for guidance, strength, and comfort during any life transition. We are reminded in Psalm 91:11 (NLT): *For he will order his angels to protect you wherever you go.* Watching my special friend settle in and trust God in transition has been beautiful to witness.

What unnecessary things have been boxed up that need to be released to move forward?

Summer

Seed

So neither the one who plants, nor the one who waters is anything, but only God can make things grow. 1 Corinthians 3:7 (NIV)

*M*any of Jesus' parables have to do with spiritual parallels to planting and farming. Our life is also like a spiritual garden. Everything starts as a seed: a relationship, an idea, even our surroundings. Nothing happens until the seed is first planted. We all travel different roads. Sadly, many of us miss opportunities to bring added beauty to our lives and to those around us.

A perfect example is John Hand, a mail carrier who traveled in his truck on a fifty-mile daily route. The drive was drab, the terrain plain and barren. One day he decided to toss wildflower seeds out his window, hoping to change the view. Today if you travel that route in the Los Altos Hills, you'll see layers of wildflowers in many vibrant colors along the roadside, which lift the spirits of all who pass by.

The beautiful things that bloom always start with the seeds we plant and when we plant them. The same is true in our own lives. We do our part: plant the seed, water, weed, and fertilize. However, we do not make the seed grow. That happens only by God's gracious work. Like a farmer, we must diligently tend to the ground and sow what God has entrusted to us. Planting is an act of faith and trust in God. Doing so moves the results out of our hands and into God's.

The Bible teaches that our words and actions are the seeds we plant. Keep planting seeds of grace, joy, love, kindness, goodness, and water them faithfully. God will make them grow in His timing.

What seeds are you spreading?

Worship

Let us go to His dwelling place, let us worship at his footstool.
Psalm 132:7

Last night our church, The Church of Eleven22, had a beautiful evening of praise and worship led by Michael Olson. While singing I felt transformed by God's limitless grace and passionate pursuit. In worship, our hearts become soft, aware, and open to the glorious majesties of God's nearness.

Throughout Scripture, music has been demonstrated to be a gift or blessing from God. Through this gift we can render praise and thanksgiving to Him. Ephesians 5:19 reminds us to sing and make melody to the Lord with our heart. It is to Him and about Him that we sing. Singing has such a unique way of bringing our heart, soul, and mind together to focus entirely on God. The apostle Paul instructed the Colossians: *Let the word of Christ dwell in you richly; teach and admonish one another in all wisdom; and with gratitude in your heart sing psalms, hymns, and spiritual songs to God. (Matthew 26:30)*

Hymns are expressions of praise to God for Who He is and for what He has done. The harp as a Christian symbol represents music, instruments, joy, and worship and praising God. The music of David's harp helped King Saul to be comforted from the tormenting spirit. David would play his harp and sing beautiful praises to God. Genuine worship music allows the Lord to fill our hearts and minds with His presence. It has a profound ability to reach past our limited understanding and help connect us to God.

There is no better way to praise the Lord than by singing, serving, and sharing the Gospel.

Service

Each of you should use whatever gift you have received to serve others, as faithful stewards of God's grace in various forms. 1 Peter 4:10 (NIV)

My dad, Bill Easterday, was an active member of Rotary International. Rotary is a nonpolitical and nonreligious global organization of over 1.4 million leaders and problem solvers who see a world in which people unite and take action to create change. Rotary's motto is "Service Above Self," and that's the way my dad lived. For sixty-five years he was an active Rotarian and served a term as their president and in other leadership roles.

He was also a recipient of the Paul Harris Fellow award, given to a Rotarian who has made an outstanding contribution to their community. Dad started a literacy campaign and the Learn to Read program in Jacksonville, in honor of Tommy—a teen who didn't know how to read until my dad helped him. Dad would take me along to the elementary schools, donating books, reading to young students, and promoting the importance of learning to read. I'm not sure it's possible to be closer as a father and daughter than we were.

Dad felt a responsibility to Rotary, his family, community, and country. He chose to bless others by serving them and God. Though I miss him dearly, I know when he entered the gates of Heaven, he was greeted by our Lord, Who said, "Well done, my good and faithful servant."

One day I know Dad and I will be reunited, and I will share with him the outcome of his legacy as a faithful servant for Christ.

How can you serve others?

Standing

Be on your guard; stand firm in the faith; be courageous; be strong. 1 Corinthians 16:13 (NIV)

Do you enjoy participating in sports? I love playing tennis and for years have enjoyed being a member of the same competitive team. What a blessing to be surrounded and supported by these amazing ladies on and off the tennis court. Many of my teammates are collegiate athletes and much more skilled than I am, yet always eager to help improve the game. Our captain, Julie, played at the Air Force Academy. She is a true leader and always offers great advice and tips which apply not only to tennis, but also to life.

Julie recently shared the importance of court position. Where we stand on the court helps determine whether or not we keep the ball in play, if we are on offense or defense, and if we can win the point. We can't control what's on the other side of the net; however, we can control where we choose to stand. Do we stand back at the baseline? Shift left or right? Charge the net? Or get caught in no man's land?

Her advice also applies to life. In tennis, we plan our shots, practice, and prepare, hoping for a positive outcome. In life, we can use the same strategy. Where we choose to stand will be evidence of the role Christ plays in our life. If we are positioned correctly and rely on God, trusting in Him and not leaning on our own understanding, He will see us through. As found in Isaiah 54:17 (NIV), *No weapon forged against you will prevail*. Like in tennis, He will help us handle any obstacle that comes our way when we stand firm with Him.

Where do you choose to stand when facing opponents?

Rest

Come to me, all who are weary and burdened, and I will give you rest. Matthew 11:28

To rest sounds so easy, but sometimes it requires supernatural strength. When I was getting everything together for a last-minute substitute teaching job, I found myself rushing around and scrambling to head out the door. I stopped and paused, realizing I needed to slow down: to settle down and take a break and a breath to prepare myself for the task at hand.

Rest is defined as "peace, ease, or refreshment." The Bible speaks quite highly of rest. It's repeated throughout Scripture, beginning with the creation story in Genesis 1 and 2. We see that God created for six days straight and then He rested on the seventh.

God commands us to lay down our burdens and spiritually rest our souls in Him. Rest is so important. In rest, our souls are restored, replenished, and filled. In rest, we are able to take time to be thankful and celebrate what God has helped us accomplish, rather than always bearing the burden of the never-ending list of tasks before us.

We think once we get this or do that, we will be content and able to rest. True rest is received, not achieved. Rest is a grace-filled reminder that we are dependent on God. We can rest confidently, knowing the unchanging God of all creation is taking care of us.

We can find refreshment and rest for our soul through prayer, being still, and reading Scripture. What worry, concern, burden, or anxiety are you carrying, that doesn't belong to you and only Jesus can carry?

"Godwinks"

Give, and it will be given to you. A good measure, pressed down, shaken together and running over will be poured into your lap. For with the measure you use, it will be measured to you. Luke 6:38 (NIV)

There is a blessing when we reflect on God's goodness, mercy, grace, and love. And how He "winks" at us at unexpected times. A "Godwink" (a term coined by author SQuire Rushnell) is an event which may seem like a coincidence, but in reality is an astonishing sign of divine intervention—especially when it seems to answer a prayer. Appreciating and reflecting on this daily will surely enrich and inspire us to count and recognize our blessings, even in difficult times.

My precious mom went to be with Jesus three years ago. It's not by chance that the owner of a small diner where I was having lunch had fresh daisies on every table. She said it was the first time she had ever put fresh flowers on the tables and something had drawn her to daisies at the floral shop. I smiled and said, "I think I know why you were drawn to the daisies. It might have been for me. My mother's name is Della and we called her Miss Daisy because it was her favorite flower. She could no longer drive, and my precious dad drove her everywhere—*Driving Miss Daisy*." The owner smiled like she understood, and before I left she gave me a hug and handed me a cluster of daisies.

It was a beautiful "Godwink" and a good reminder that God gives freely to us so we may freely bless others. I am grateful for my new sweet friend for sharing God's goodness with an open heart and a handful of daisies.

Distractions

Do not be conformed to this world but be transformed by the renewal of your mind, that by testing you may discern what is the will of God, what is good and acceptable and perfect. Romans 12:2 (NIV)

Recently when I was traveling, the captain shared that air traffic control put a hold on all flights so we wouldn't have to circle in midair. I thought about how this can relate to our thought life. Thoughts circle above, coming in and out. If one lands, it's because we gave it permission. If one leaves, it's because we directed it out. We can select our thought pattern.

Developing a habit of watchfulness over our thinking is a discipline that will change our lives and protect our minds. We can't always control our circumstances or distractions, but we can control what we think of them. If you don't like your circumstances, find a new way to think about them. Change the channel! With the spirit and Word of God, we can renew our minds. God allows us to walk in safety since the Word of God is a *lamp to my feet and a light to my path. (Psalm 119:105)* Just as a lamp shines to guide our steps, God's Word illuminates and guides our way.

Pastor Rick Warren said, "Manage your mind, because it's the key to peace and happiness." An unmanaged mind leads to conflict and turbulence. A managed mind leads to strength, security, and serenity. The Word of God is a tremendous help since the Bible contains God's thoughts. When thoughts start circling, ask yourself, Is it true and good? Blessed and holy? If not, let it go. When the Holy Spirit controls our minds, the results are peaceful, joyful, and enduring.

Caregiving Compassion

Therefore, as God's chosen people, holy and dearly loved, clothe yourselves with compassion, kindness, humility, gentleness and patience. Colossians 3:12 (NIV)

While visiting my precious mom in memory care at HarborChase of Jacksonville, I witnessed her caregivers and other associates deliver nurturing, tender care that went above and beyond any job description. Respectfully managing memory care issues is no easy task; however, they provided stimulating, compassionate care in a secure and loving environment.

I have used the words compassion, sympathy, and empathy—sometimes interchangeably. All three words are related to the idea of seeing and understanding what another person is feeling. But with compassion, there is an added step of relieving the pain a person is experiencing. The tenderness demonstrated by the simple act of holding a resident's hand during a visit, blossoms into comfort and compassion.

A person who develops a legacy of compassion sees and takes action to help meet the needs of others—with no agenda. When we look for ways to demonstrate compassion toward others, we are cultivating a legacy of compassion.

A heart of compassion comes authentically, naturally, and effortlessly through a God-centered life. As we draw closer to Him through His Word, He transforms our focus, thoughts, and feelings. Are you aware that the seemingly random coincidences popping up during the course of our days might actually be divine encounters? These could be God-given opportunities to see and act with compassion.

Are you open and willing?

Inspire

I praise you, for you are fearfully and wonderfully made. Wonderful are your works, my soul knows it very well. Psalm 139:14

Join me and let this Scripture penetrate your soul.

McKenzie Noelle Wilson, in her short life, inspired everyone she touched with her beautiful spirit, love for Christ, and unconditional love. Although McKenzie was called home to be with the Lord at the age of 15, she affected more lives than others do in a lifetime through her random acts of kindness, charity, and love toward those in need. This was the inspiration behind the foundation created in her honor and Camp Kenzie.

As Camp Kenzie at the Boys & Girls Clubs comes to a close this summer, my heart is full. This was the tenth year of our Girl Time. During Girl Time we have shared, loved, danced, and learned what it means to let your light shine. These special ladies have grown so much in their self-confidence, and their inner beauty radiates. What a joy to witness them take the runway and model beautiful outfits donated by Hope's Closet. The girls recognize they are beautiful and they are fearfully and wonderfully made by God. Today's culture talks about love and where to find it, rather than demonstrating it.

The ripple effect of love, self-confidence, and kindness that began with the words McKenzie circled in her Bible and by the way she lived, continues to touch so many lives … especially mine.

What inspiring ripple effect are you passing along to others?

Generosity

Whoever brings blessing will be enriched, and one who waters will himself be watered. Proverbs 11:25

The spirit of generosity can reach deeply into every corner of our lives. True generosity is giving from the heart; it is the giving of ourselves through our demonstration of love, time, compassion, and kindness, with no strings or demands attached. It's way more than material possessions. Generosity comes from what's stored up in our hearts, including love, gratitude, and joy. Whoever refreshes others will be refreshed.

Harry Dandison Dewey—otherwise known as Dan, the coffee man—has been giving, with no end in sight. For many years he's delivered Starbucks coffee to the Rose Cancer Center at Beaumont Hospital in Detroit. He began the tradition when his father was getting chemotherapy. During one session, Dan got up for coffee for his dad and offered to get some for others. After he saw how happy it made the people receiving treatment, he decided to keep it up.

Dan shared: "It's about keeping God in the center of your life and blessing and loving others." He asks for nothing in return. Dan is a retired audiovisual specialist from the public school system, and began spending upward of $10,000 on coffee and other drinks for strangers. "Doing good creates more good," he said. It became his mission, errand of mercy, and calling. When he brought his dad home after chemo, his dad said, "Keep going, son. Keep delivering coffee and keep spreading joy." Generosity is not something that shows up; it's a lifestyle you cultivate, regardless of what's in your wallet.

Unify

Behold, how good and pleasant it is when brothers dwell in unity! Psalm 133:1

Summer is one of my favorite seasons. It's a season of warmth and relaxation, a time of freedom and refreshment. Flowers are in full bloom, and as the sunshine stretches to make the days longer, everything becomes even brighter and more cheerful. Summer is a great time to experience the joy that living in Christ brings, allowing us to enjoy all which God provides. As we experience God's gifts through the beauty of nature and simple pleasures with friends, our joy and gratefulness are multiplied.

Many of my wonderful childhood memories feature bike rides. The one thing which surpasses overall is the gift of riding bikes with friends and family. It's a good way to invest in our relationships. Unity is a beautiful thing to experience: it's enjoyable and reveals God's presence. It brings blessings to us and to others since it satisfies a thirst we all desperately need, whether on a bike or not.

While biking with my children, we talked about all the fun opportunities summer brings. We shared laughter and enjoyed the simple pleasures of God's creation surrounding us as we pedaled away. Riding together, enjoying His fingerprints through the uphills and downhills and twists and turns can be compared to the events in our lives, which are always better with those we treasure beside us.

Ready for a bike ride?

Journey

Enter through the narrow gate. For wide is the gate and broad is the road that leads to destruction, and many enter through it. But small is the gate and narrow the road that leads to life, and only a few find it. Matthew 7:13-14

As we think about our life's journey, sometimes we don't know which way to go … yet God does. Life can be full of wrong turns, missed opportunities, and poor decisions throwing us easily off the correct path. We're left to wonder how long it will take to get back on track. The good news is God uses even the wrong turns and wrong roads to lead us to the right place.

While driving in an unfamiliar city, I found myself lost. Thank goodness for my GPS system. Even when I made a wrong turn, it recalculated, sending me in the correct direction. In life, I've witnessed God do the same. When I take a wrong turn, He is there to recalculate my journey, setting me back on the correct path—His path. Even when we can't see what's around the corner, we can trust that we are in the hands of the one who made the map.

I love that no matter where we are, God is already there. I also love the thought that sometimes He will carry us when we are too tired to continue on our own. Psalm 16:11 assures us that when we abide in Him, God will lead us forward in His plans for our lives: *You make known the path of life, you will fill me with joy and your presence, with eternal pleasures at your right hand.*

Remember, if you're headed in the wrong direction, God allows U-turns. If you've veered off your path, don't be afraid to recalculate.

Sharing

Do not neglect to do good and to share what you have, for such sacrifices are pleasing to God. Hebrews 13:16

Hebrews 13:16 teaches us to help those in need, sacrifice our time, and, with compassionate hearts, share our resources freely so that God may be glorified. Sharing is an essential social skill to build healthy, strong relationships, and it contributes to both our well-being and the well-being of others.

We must be careful. Without realizing it, our lives can become too busy or so self-centered that we close ourselves off to others' needs. This lifestyle is selfish, unsatisfying, and eventually leads to loneliness. Making room for God and for other people is an intentional lifestyle.

While at the Boys and Girls Clubs camp, I watched how the kids were snapping apart their twin popsicles. Purple was the favorite and there were not enough to go around. So as one camper snapped hers to share, others followed and the sharing became contagious.

Have you ever noticed when marketers want to show how enjoyable their products are—from pizza and popcorn to Kit Kat bars—the images are always about people sharing? So is the way many products are packaged, such as two Reese's Peanut Butter Cups—one for you and one for your friend. Our souls become more nurtured through sharing.

One day when we stand before God, He won't ask the square footage of our home, but He will ask how many people we welcomed into our home to share a meal or fellowship. He won't ask us how many friends we had, but He will ask how many people to whom we were a friend.

What are you willing to share?

Soar

But those who hope in the Lord will renew their strength. They will soar on wings. Like eagles, they will run and not grow weary, they will walk and not be faint. Isaiah 40:31

To my amazement, I recently witnessed an eagle in my front yard. It seemed to be in search of something it possibly had dropped in the grass. I'd never seen an eagle up close and was stunned by its powerful build, beauty, and majesty. I was especially awed when it took off and soared away into the sky.

The Bible mentions eagles more than thirty times. Eagles balance aggression with gracefulness. They soar without flapping their wings. They are the symbol of courage and faith. When we feel we need strength, God in heaven knows our burdens. He can carry the loads of life and never grow weary. Rather than relying on our own strengths, by putting our hope in the Lord we let Him lift our burdens and carry us through so we, too, can soar through life like an eagle.

The acronym SOAR is a beautiful example. S – Scripture: Take our time reading God's Word. O – Observation: What is God revealing to us in this particular passage? A – Application: How does this apply to our life right now? R – Respond: to Scripture with a personal commitment to apply it and trust God to help us. By doing this, we can then SOAR above any circumstances, knowing and trusting He will carry us through.

What do you need to surrender to God so that you can SOAR?

Love Lives Here

"You shall love the Lord your God with all your heart, and with all your soul, and with all your mind, and with all your strength." The second is this, "You shall love your neighbor as yourself." There is no greater commandment than these. Mark 12:30-31

Jesus said the most important thing we should do is love God and love others. If we look around, we see so many people are lonely and empty. What's missing? I believe life is not full until we let God in to fill it.

So many times, we search for satisfaction and meaning in worldly things. However, no amount of money, accomplishments, alcohol, popularity, or prestige will ever be enough. God gives us living water. He also gives us connections with others. As followers of Christ, we are called to nurture, protect, and build our relationships so God is glorified.

I just read, for the second time, the book *Love Lives Here*, by Maria Goff. It's about finding what you need in a world telling you what you want. It inspired and challenged me to hold a mirror up to my life. Maria reminds us that our job is to use our gifts to the best of our abilities and to declare love lives here.

When we put God first and love others, we are choosing to drink from His well of living water instead of dipping into the shallow wells of the world. Our love for Christ can be seen in our attitudes and behaviors toward others. Genuine love flows from God Who dwells within us. Are you able to say, "Love lives here"?

Walk by Faith

For we walk by faith, not by sight. 2 Corinthians 5:7

I love to walk outside. It started while pregnant with my daughter Tori, as a way to keep healthy. I didn't realize the benefits walking would provide so many years later. Living in Pittsburgh at the time—whether in sunshine, rain, or snow—away I'd go. Walking alone or with friends, I made it a daily lifelong habit and a wonderful way to appreciate nature and spend time with God, surrounded by His blessings. Walking requires us to get up and get started. It involves motivation, motion, and moving for a purpose. Studies have proven walking outdoors improves our mind, health, happiness, and soul.

However, we can walk by sight or by faith. We all know what it means to walk by sight. To walk by faith, we must be engaged and consistent. Walking by faith requires us to trust and believe that God is preparing us for blessings and relief from whatever trials we are facing. It means rejoicing and praising Him through hard times, knowing and trusting that God is in control. It means giving up our desire to navigate our own lives and placing our faith and trust in Him.

The Bible tells us that even when the path ahead does not appear certain or what we intended, we must choose to walk by faith. In Hebrews 11:1 (NIV), we're reminded: *Now faith is confidence in what we hope for and assurance about what we do not see.* This unseen power is God Himself.

How do you walk?

Wonders

I will praise you, O Lord, with all my heart; I will tell of your wonders. I will be glad and rejoice in you; I will sing praise to your name, O Most High. Psalm 9:1-2

Everyone needs a dose of goodness. Well, that is what I experienced by spending time with the brother of my wonderful friend Marla. Marc's love for Jesus and others is inspiring and contagious. While talking about the wonders of the world, he told us the present wonders for him are things most people take for granted, like being able to see and hear. Marc needs hearing aids to hear and glasses to see. While at the beach he said without them he could not hear the ocean, birds, and laughter, or see the waves and beautiful boats on the horizon. He said wonders are simple things, special people, and that God created us all in His own unique way. He noticed so many people miss out on the beauty of God's creation because they take the simple things in life for granted: to hear, see, walk, feel, touch, laugh, and, most of all, to love.

Marc acts out of true goodness of his heart. His actions come from a place of selflessness. When we act out of true goodness and reflect the fruit of the Spirit, we are obedient to God's commandments and want to bless others. Goodness is not about doing elaborate things to gain recognition. Sometimes the small acts of sharing awareness mean the most.

One thing is for sure: I left him with my heart overflowing and a great reminder that things we overlook as simply ordinary are truly wondrous.

What simple wonders are you taking for granted?

Honey

But he would feed you with the finest of the wheat, and with honey from the rock I would satisfy you. Psalm 81:16

In this verse, we see that God provides us everything we need, even from sources where we least expect it. In the third chapter of Exodus when God called Moses to lead the slaves out of Egypt, He told him to lead them into a land that would flow with milk and honey. Honey in the rock, in the Bible, invokes a clear and creative picture of God's sweet goodness in places we don't expect to find it. God's Word is the honey in the rock and He is the rock of our salvation. What He promises He will also perform.

My daughter Tori and I love to go to Christian concerts together. It's a special way we bond and worship. At a recent concert we were moved by the song "Honey in the Rock," by Brooke Ligertwood and Brandon Lake. It reminds us that when we are faithful, we don't need to harbor worries because God is always next to us and provides us with what we need.

Being faithful means relying on God in good times and in moments of difficulties. This song paints a beautiful picture of God's provisions, such as giving manna to the Israelites in the desert and bringing water out of a stone to quench their thirst.

What comfort we have when we fully trust God's plan for us. Even when we only see rocks around us, we know He will provide, even if it means placing honey in the rock.

Upon reflection, where have you experienced the sweetness of honey in the rock?

Mentoring

Whatever you have learned or received, or heard from me, or seen in me, put into practice. And the God of peace will be with you. Philippians 4:9 (NIV)

A mentor could be defined as "a friend or spiritual role model with a serving, giving, and encouraging attitude of humility." Jesus is our primary mentoring role model. He empowers and transforms us through equipping, enabling, and anointing us. God has a heart for mentoring. Throughout the Bible, we see the idea of teaching through relationship by the examples of Naomi to Ruth, Moses to Joshua, and Paul to Timothy. Mentoring is a result of relationships. It's a process of imparting love, encouragement, and wisdom, and involves honesty, giving, and sharing.

I've been blessed by many wonderful mentors in my life and have had the opportunity to mentor at the Boys & Girls Clubs at summer camp, over the last ten years, through "Girl Time." It's been beautiful to witness their transformation. Each year we spend time on the importance of kindness, character, friendship, trust, confidence, and inner beauty. Through caring, giving, and growing, these teenagers are learning to recognize and reach their full potential. Camp closes with a fashion show in honor of McKenzie Wilson, who was a role model to many in her short life.

What a blessing it is to be a part of the Boys & Girls Clubs, sharing and teaching them some of the beautiful things that have been passed along to me through mentors.

What mentoring opportunities can you put into practice?

Mountains

I lift up my eyes to the mountain, where does my help come from? My help comes from the Lord, the maker of heaven and earth. Psalm 121:1 (NIV)

In the Bible, mountains are mentioned 570 times. They convey power and strength. They can symbolize an obstacle. They are considered holy places and used for religious purposes. The term mountaintop experience comes from those moments in the Bible when God revealed Himself to people on a mountain. Some are: the Sermon on the Mount, where Jesus delivered the Beatitudes; Mount Sinai, where the Ten Commandments were revealed to Moses; and Mount Ararat, where Noah's ark came to rest after the Flood. Mountains represent both God as our refuge and the obstacles we face in life. Mountains are constant and unmoving, which is why they are a powerful imagery used in the Bible to depict God's power over everything.

The Great Smoky Mountains are often referred to as "God's country." After many visits to Tennessee with my parents and family, I now know why. The majestic mountains draw you closer to nature and Christ. My dad was born and raised in Knoxville, Tennessee, and loved to share his roots of faith and passion for the Smokies. His favorite spot was called Cades Cove. It's impossible to visit Cades Cove without feeling a deep sense of wonder.

Watching horses graze in a wide-open field while the sun shines lightly on the mountains is sure to take your breath away. I felt a sense of holiness surrounding me. Mountains draw us closer to Christ, and, as in life, the best view is attained after the hardest climb.

Friendship

Perfume and incense make the heart glad, but the sweetness of a friend is a fragrant forest. Proverbs 27:9 (GWT)

Friendship is a God-ordained and blessed relationship. Proverbs 12:26 tells us that the righteous choose their friends carefully. Good friends are one of God's greatest gifts. Not one of us is meant to go through life alone and without help. God longs to use us as His hands and feet, in order to bless others and extend the reach of His Kingdom. Living sacrificially, without an agenda or motive in our friendships, is the most peaceful and joyful way to live.

While with special friends on our annual summer's girls tennis retreat at Clear Lake, Indiana, this was evident—not only by our generous hostess, Barb, but by the circle of friends surrounding me. We stand united, encouraging laughter and joy, praying together, and being grateful for both the beautiful surroundings and our special time together. Many years of pure and authentic friendship built on the foundation of faith have created a strong bond among us, in which Christ is the center and joy is contagious, even in difficult circumstances.

A special Clear Lake resident and new friend, Susan, delivered homemade treats for us and others, and then whizzed off on her bike, spreading her joy to others. While dealing with her loved one's health issues and needs, Susan still found a way to bless others. She's not focusing on her own circumstances, but on Christ and being a fountain and a light, and trusting God. Her kindness and generosity to all are like a fragrant forest surrounding Clear Lake.

Where can you spread your kindness and generosity?

Praise

May all who seek you rejoice and be glad in you; may those who love your salvation say continually, "Great is the Lord." Psalm 40:16

The Psalms are songs of praise to God as our Creator, sustainer, and Redeemer. Focusing our thoughts on God moves us to praise Him. The more we know Him, the more we can appreciate what He has done for us.

Listening to Chris Tomlin in concert sing "How Great Is Our God" turned my attention to the greatness of God's power, holiness, and mercy. Chris said he wrote this song while sitting in his apartment in Austin, strumming his guitar and reading the Psalms. The lyrics of his worship song start by addressing just how wonderful our God is.

What follows is a simple call to action as to how we should respond to His greatness: Rejoice in glory as we proclaim … how great is our God!

Of Chris Tomlin's new song, "Holy Forever," he said, "There are songs of deliverance which, when it comes to worship, those are the songs of rescue—like Lord, I need you, rescue me." Tomlin described that we need those songs, but there are also songs of transcendence in which we take our eyes off ourselves and focus on the glory of God. In his song "Holy Forever," Chris then invites us to engage in something far bigger than us: eternal worship.

Listen to his songs, "How Great Is Our God" and "Holy Forever," and meditate on the holiness of God. You will be blessed.

Summer

Our mouths were filled with laughter, our tongues with songs of joy. Then it was said among the nations, "The Lord has done great things for them." Psalm 126:2 (NIV)

For most of us, summer boosts our energy and mood and represents the height of positivity, action, and adventure. This season can be a time to interrupt structure and bring a playful change in routine, with more outdoor time and fun activities with family and friends.

Although there were hot days, thunderstorms, and mosquito bites, I remember the simple pleasures and joy summer brought while growing up: family barbecues, sprinklers, slip and slides, lemonade stands, and watermelon. There were trips to the lake, boat rides, hiking, bike rides, and games of hide-and-seek. These are adventures I experienced with my children too, hoping to pass along the blessings of simple pleasures and the value of relationships.

Through all the fun and games of summer, Vacation Bible School was a highlight that drew my children closer to God and each other. My parents instilled in me the importance of a close sibling relationship. When we tattled on each other or disagreed, they told us to work it out. My brother Billy has been and will always be one of my best friends and wise mentors.

As we experience God's hand through the beauty of nature—beaches, mountains, sunsets, and blue skies—let's remember Who created it and be grateful for His beautiful gifts and not take them for granted. No matter your age, nothing compares to the joy of experiencing this season, surrounded by God's creation and those you love.

How do you enjoy summer?

Giving

Do not withhold good from those to whom it is due, when it is in your power to act. Proverbs 3:27 (NIV)

My friend Corey, a firefighter and entrepreneur, told me how a client, out of the blue, blessed him with a trip to the Bahamas. Corey prayed that one day he could take his wife on a special vacation. Then his client surprised him with this trip. He told Corey it is because he has been blessed and wants to bless others. Corey said this same busy man is being a mentor to him and helping him with long-term business goals. He didn't disclose who it was because the man wanted no worldly credit.

This is a good reminder that true servants don't serve for the approval or applause of others; they are content to live for an audience of one. They are content with serving God.

It is clear if we begin giving ourselves to others, sharing what we have—our time, knowledge, talent, love, and treasures—and not focusing on what we don't have but on what we are blessed with, we will find ourselves in a place of peaceful contentment.

Choosing to help others will give us an appreciation not only for who we are and the blessings we have, but more importantly, to serve God by serving others. The Bible reminds us: a self-centered man is a discontented man. In contrast, the soul of the generous man, the man who truly lives for the interests and benefit of others, will find blessing upon blessing in his own life.

Today, stop and ask yourself if you are truly content. If not, who can you bless with your giving?

Drifting

Therefore we must pay much closer attention to what we have heard, lest we drift away from it. Hebrews 2:1

While taking a walk on the beach, I saw a large piece of driftwood covered with moss and debris. It apparently had been tossed and tumbled in the sea and left alone on the shoreline. I wondered where it had drifted from.

Drift is defined as "a gradual shift in position, an aimless course, to be carried along subject to no guidance or control." Drifting happens when we fail to pay attention. It's not done deliberately. It's seldom a sudden process. Drifting is deceptive. It occurs slowly, is hardly recognizable, and requires no effort. People may drift from God in search of more—more freedom, fun, choices, and pleasure.

What seems to begin as fun and pleasure can easily end in a shipwreck because we've drifted along, neglecting to notice how fast we're moving away from the safety of the Lord's plan. We can get swept up and drift away when storms, trials, and persecutions overtake us, instead of clinging to and paying attention to the Word of God.

"Pay attention" was used in the early Greek language to mean to hold course by securing your anchor. No wind, storm, or fear can cause us to drift away when we are anchored in Christ. The book of Hebrews says that if we do not pay attention to the Word of God, we will drift away.

Don't get swept away by the world's currents. We can avoid drifting away from God by staying anchored to the rock. He will never leave us or forsake us. God provides an anchor for our soul.

Fall

Joyful

A joyful heart is good medicine, but a crushed spirit dries up the bones. Proverbs 17:22

While I was visiting with friends, joy became the topic of our conversation. In order to truly declare to the world Who our Heavenly Father is, we should be carriers of joy: joy which comes from our all-powerful, all-knowing, and all-loving God.

My dad always reminded me that no one can steal my joy unless I let them, especially when I was going through trials or difficulties. He shared from the Bible that wisdom leads to joy, and we will find this path from wisdom to joy when we trust and follow God. *For wisdom will enter your heart, and knowledge will fill you with joy. Proverbs 2:10 (NLT)* We can feel joy regardless of what is happening or not happening in our lives because joy comes from God— the source of all joy. As we spread joy, it multiplies and is contagious.

God wants to deposit a resilient hope in our heart, not shallow happiness which melts in the heat of adversity. A joyful person chooses to see God at work, even in their trials. God gives us the power to change atmospheres, to brighten someone's day, to break off heaviness, and to lead others to a deeper revelation of His goodness when we reflect His joy to others. No circumstance, trial, or worldly stress can steal the joy God has placed within us. Don't let a crushed spirit dry up your bones. Instead … choose to be joyful!

Difficulties

Your word is a lamp unto my feet and a light unto my path.
Psalm 119:105

While driving my dad up to my brother and sister-in-law's lake house to celebrate Dad's 89th birthday, we encountered lane closures, detours, and potholes. Toward the end of our eight-hour journey we passed a small country church with a marquee which read: WITH THE LORD, DIFFICULT ROADS OFTEN LEAD TO BEAUTIFUL DESTINATIONS

As I sat by the peaceful lake this morning I reflected on those words. We naturally hope to avoid difficult roads in life; we want the beautiful destinations without difficulties. With the Lord, His Word, and the Holy Spirit guiding us around every bump in the road, we will ultimately make it through any terrain. God is moving behind the scenes, bringing order out of chaos, shifting, sifting, and positioning us.

We all go through hard times when it seems staying down is a whole lot easier than getting back up to fight another day. A good quote to remember is: "Falling down is an accident; staying down is a choice." In Psalm 16:11 we are reminded, *You make known to me the path of life; You will fill me with joy in your presence, with eternal pleasures at your right hand*. Choose to follow God, knowing that on His path we will be in His presence and filled with His joy. He puts us on the right path for the purpose of His Kingdom.

There are many unexpected surprises and divine difficulties which bless, connect, and protect, that are actually setups, not setbacks. What difficulties can you reflect on now, realizing it was a setup and not a setback?

Purse

Every word of God proves true; he is a shield to those who take refuge in him. Proverbs 30:5

Like the Capital One commercial "What's in your wallet?" you can learn a lot about a woman from the contents of her purse. Some are well organized, and then there's me. I would have been a good contestant on the TV game show *Let's Make a Deal*. Monty Hall would have found many treasures during his segment "What's in My Bag?" I have everything from aspirin and hairspray, to sermon church notes scribbled on old receipts, and a few candy wrappers too. My travel tote and suitcase are much the same. I always travel with a candle and bubble bath in my suitcase to remind me of home, and, in my tote, my Bible, chargers, and earphones are important. But there are always unimportant items which need to be trashed. I smiled and thought about this as I cleaned out both my purse and tote bag.

Sometimes the good things we carry can get crowded out by the junk we need to discard. In Psalm 119:11, we read: *I have hidden your word in my heart that I might not sin against you. (NIV)* When God's Word resides in us, rather than digging through to find the truth about who we are and what truly matters (like weeding through the clutter of my purse), we get to the good—God's Word. As we read it, study it, and tuck it into our hearts, we can activate, access, and apply it easily. We become what we behold. I love Charles Spurgeon's quote: "Nearness to God brings likeness to God. The more you see God the more of God will be seen in you."

What do you need to clean out in order to seek refuge in God?

Gratitude

Give thanks in all circumstances, for this is the will of God in Christ Jesus for you. 1 Thessalonians 5:18

During a Sunday sermon, Pastor Joby Martin delivered a beautiful message on gratefulness and the importance of writing a gratitude list. We're quick to write grocery lists and to-do lists, but how often do we actually start or end our day with a gratitude list?

Thankfulness is one of the most powerful tools in making our hearts both soft to the seed of God's Word and filled with abundant joy. Cultivating a spirit of gratitude honors God and strengthens our faith. Gratefulness breeds joy and trust rather than entitlement and negativity.

Many of us consider gratitude to be a feeling, but in Scripture, gratitude is action. In at least 162 places in the Bible, God references His desire for us to show gratitude. Jesus began and ended His prayers with words of thanks and praise to God. In the Lord's Prayer, He taught His followers to do the same.

Think about our conversations: Are they marked by complaints or gratitude? What's in our heart will eventually spill out to those around us. A heartfelt "Thank you" are two of the most important words we can say. Gratitude glorifies God. It can take time to harvest a fruitful spirit of joy. One of the best ways to cultivate joy is to practice gratitude, choosing to be thankful to God and to others.

A friend asked me this: "What if you wake up tomorrow with only the things you thanked God for today?"

Do you have a gratitude list?

Renewal

And to be renewed in the spirit of your minds. Ephesians 4:23

While traveling I noticed the battery was low on my cell phone, so I went to plug it into a power source to charge. However, since I was traveling abroad, I didn't have the correct adapter. There I sat with a soon-to-be dead battery and the wrong power source. I thought about how electronics are useless if their power source cannot be charged or if they're plugged into the wrong source.

In the same way, this holds true in our lives—it matters what we are plugged into. Without the spiritual power God gives us and our staying connected to Him, we won't be as effective. Sometimes we need to stop, be still, and renew our attitudes and mindsets. Romans 12:2 reminds us to be transformed by the renewing of our mind. Like a battery needs to be charged and sometimes changed, we must turn to Him, get plugged into His Word, and, through prayer, connect and recharge. Allowing God to fill us up with the Holy Spirit is the best form of renewal.

When my kids were growing up and bad thoughts entered their young minds, I reminded them to change the channel and plug into God's Word, all of which is available by faith. Living differently begins with thinking differently. What a gift to accept and rest in! *Therefore, since we have been justified by faith, we have peace with God through our Lord Jesus Christ. Romans 5:1*

What power source are you plugged into? Is it time to change the channel?

Rescue

Because he holds fast to me in love, I will deliver him; I will protect him because he knows my name. Psalm 91:14

The word *rescue* is a strong word from the Hebrew language. It paints the picture of an individual who is helpless and cannot deliver himself in an oppressive situation. One of my favorite songs is "Rescue Story," written and sung by Zach Williams. All of us have a rescue story to share. Zach Williams certainly does. My daughter took me to one of his concerts, and I'm still reflecting on his amazing music and testimony.

He grew up in a Christian home, but went through years of rebellion. He dropped out of high school and started a rock and roll band. He was living hard and fast, but still felt empty inside. After hearing Big Daddy Weave's "Redeemed" on the radio—a song based on the power of redemption—Zach made the decision that he had run from God long enough. The musician surrendered his life to Christ and walked away from what our world claims is fame and fortune, into his new life. He said the peace he found is indescribable. He said God was always there waiting patiently for him to surrender. Zach's career continues to flourish as a Grammy Award–winning Contemporary Christian artist.

The song lyrics say it all: "You were the voice in the desert, calling me out in the dead of night. Fighting my battles for me, you are my rescue story. Jesus lifted us out of the ashes and carried our souls from death to life; bringing us from glory to glory; you are my rescue story." He ended the concert by saying, "If your life has not been changed yet, tonight can be the night your rescue story starts."

Optimism

May the God of hope fill you with all joy and peace as you trust in him, so that you may overflow with hope by the power of the Holy Spirit. Romans 15:13

God has great plans for our lives. We can choose to be optimistic, confident, and courageous through Christ.

God doesn't want us to be backward-looking. We get stuck when we ruminate on negative thoughts, people, or situations. I was reminded in a sermon: "Instead of cursing, nursing, and rehearsing them, we must disperse them." It takes a positive attitude to move forward. Our faith is a positive power in our life. If we are positive in our core convictions, we will be positive in our conversations with ourselves and others.

When I was growing up, my mom always reminded me, "What's down in the well comes up in the pail." She explained I shouldn't hold on to negative things or people, keep moving forward, trust in God, and don't look back. It was one of many beautiful life lessons from my precious mom. I never witnessed her in a bad mood; she had contagious laughter and a spirit of joy and adventure. With her positive attitude, she stepped out in faith, leaving behind everything familiar to her in North Dakota to settle in Florida—a reminder that optimism shines like the sun through dark clouds.

We can't control what other people do, but we can control the space in our own heart and mind. When God asks us to leave the familiar behind, let His Word encourage us to keep moving forward. It's beautiful to witness what God will do through a person who steps out in faith.

Does optimism flow from you?

Thanksgiving

O give thanks to the Lord, for He is good; for His mercy and loving-kindness endure forever! 1 Chronicles 16:34

Giving thanks is something which should occur every day of the year, not only as we prepare for Thanksgiving.

Thanksgiving is an essential element of worship—it elevates our affection for God and leads to gratitude. Gratitude is an appreciation for what you have. It grows over time and is a force which empowers us to scale greater heights. Researchers show that gratitude can lead to increased levels of happiness and satisfaction in our earthly life. The byproduct of gratitude is joy. Joy is the settled assurance that God is in control. Thus we have the quiet confidence that ultimately everything is going to be all right, and we have made the determined choice to praise God in all things. Joy is not dictated by our circumstances—it is fostered by the attitude in our hearts.

Nothing brightens life like the spirit of thanksgiving. From thankfulness comes an outpouring of gratitude that is infectious and life-giving to those around us. Gratitude paves the way for blessings in both body and soul. When we are truly grateful for God's power at work in us and God's gift of life, we cannot contain this joy. Joy and peace are the beautiful results of choosing a godly, thankful, faith-filled attitude.

Thanksgiving provokes the blessings of God upon our lives. When we thank God, we glorify His name. One of the real indications of a person's life being touched and changed by Jesus is that they overflow with thankfulness.

What one thing about this day are you grateful for?

Blessings

Taste and see that the Lord is good; blessed is the one who takes refuge in him. Psalm 34:8

The other day I heard the song "Blessings" by Laura Story. It's been around for a while, written in 2011. Laura's husband was diagnosed with brain cancer. Her journey through this trial brought her to understand their suffering as God's mercies in disguise. She tells how the blessings she received came through raindrops and tears: "'Cause what if Your blessings come through raindrops / What if Your healing comes through tears / What if a thousand sleepless nights are what it takes to know You're near."

These lyrics struck me because the blessings of God often come disguised—sometimes as a difficulty—something we would never choose for ourselves. In the midst of pain it's easy to lose sight of God. However, in retrospect we see how God's loving hand guided and directed us in such a way that our lives were enriched, strengthened, and enlarged. Laura's husband survived, but even if he hadn't, God guided her through her trial. He never abandons us.

In relationship to God, a blessing is a gift of His grace, the touch of His hand upon our life, the comfort and the breath of His presence and His strength—helping us grow closer and cling to Him rather than to our temporary circumstances. There is a blessing when we reflect on God's goodness, mercy, grace, and love. Appreciating and reflecting on this daily will surely enrich and inspire us to count and recognize our blessings even when they come through raindrops.

What raindrops can you now reflect on as blessings?

Turn Around

Come and hear, all who fear God, And I will declare what He has done for my soul. Psalm 66:16

A while back, my dad and I had the pleasure of getting together with Tyrone for dinner. We met Tyrone years ago on Father's Day when we were in line at a 7-Eleven convenience store. He seemed broken, and a casual conversation began. He told us he had just been released from serving time and was staying at the City Rescue Mission house and was determined to turn his life around. My dad, a servant for Christ, stepped in and began to mentor Tyrone to shift his focus on becoming the man God created him to be.

We continued our friendship over the years; Tyrone lovingly referred to my dad as "Pops." Watching Tyrone turn his life around has been so beautiful to witness—not only for us, but for those around him in Folkston, Georgia. Tyrone shared that while pumping gas a man told him how much he respects Tyrone for his change in lifestyle. His choices to live God's way, work hard, and tap into God through the Word, prayer, and deed are contagious to those around Tyrone.

This is a good reminder that testimonies give hope and strengthen faith. His testimony is evidence of God's faithfulness and redeeming power. Tyrone is helping believers and nonbelievers see physical evidence of what God can do in someone's life. What the enemy meant for evil, God has turned it for good.

What test has led to your testimony?

Love

Love is patient, love is kind. It does not envy, it does not boast, it is not proud. It is not rude, it is not self-seeking, it is not easily angered, it keeps no record of wrongs. Love does not delight in evil but rejoices with the truth. It always protects, always trusts, always hopes, always perseveres. Love never fails. 1 Corinthians 1:13

On a recent trip to the bank, I made a deposit and, on the same visit, I made a withdrawal. As I drove away from the building, I thought about another kind of banking we do every day—the love bank contained in our hearts. When we increase our relationship deposits we will discover how much richer our relationships will be. Love banking only happens when we are not keeping score and when we are genuinely more concerned about what we are giving than what we're receiving.

Whether we realize it or not, every word we speak to another either makes a deposit to that relationship in our love bank—or a withdrawal from it. Each critical, harsh, mean, or hurtful word spoken to another is a withdrawal from the relationship's love bank account. In time, that account becomes overdrawn and closes.

On the other side, each kind, loving, positive, encouraging, or helpful word spoken with sincerity to another is a deposit into the relationship's account in our love banks, and they both continue to grow and prosper.

We honor the Lord when our words and actions deposit positive seeds which reflect God's goodness. Let's reflect on ways to limit withdrawals and increase deposits. Why not begin today to make positive deposits in someone's love bank.

What is your love bank account balance?

Transformation

Do not conform to the pattern of this world, but be transformed by the renewing of your mind. Then you will be able to test and approve what God's will is—his good, pleasing and perfect will. Romans 12:2 (NIV)

In this Scripture, Paul urges us to be transformed from the inside out. I witnessed this firsthand through a divine encounter when I heard Khalil Osiris speak at the Boys & Girls Clubs. He is an author, speaker, and founder of Truth & Reconciliation Conversations.

After hearing his presentation, I was so inspired with his testimony that I brought my dad to meet him at Starbucks. Khalil told us he spent twenty years in prison for crimes he takes full responsibility for committing, and that for many people prison is a metaphor for self-imposed limitations. Khalil chose to make his cell his classroom and the prison his university. He obtained both his BA and MA from Boston University while there—one of only .0001 percent to do so while incarcerated. He read his Bible over seventy-five times.

Khalil put his security in the Lord, knowing his identity is in Christ Jesus. He used his time in incarceration to transform his life and energy with a deep understanding of how to use personal crises and challenges as opportunities for self-improvement and to bless others. He is described by a colleague and friend as, above all, a servant determined to reach out and make a difference worldwide, leaving his thumbprint—the character of God. As we parted, Khalil said to us, "Be the evidence of what's possible. How bright does your light shine?"

Testimonies of transformations are powerful. What thumbprints are you leaving behind?

Focus

Finally, brothers and sisters, whatever is true, whatever is noble, whatever is right, whatever is pure, whatever is lovely, whatever is admirable—if anything is excellent or praiseworthy—think on these things. Philippians 4:8 (NIV)

When I was taking a picture with my children, the lens was smudged; the picture was out of focus and blurry. Once the lens was cleaned, the picture was clear and vibrant. In life, many things can blur our focus. The good news is God has given us a way to check our internal focus to make sure it's right and healthy.

We all view life, others, and situations through a lens. What we choose to focus on through this lens determines the images we see around us. It's the perspective from which we look at things that will hugely influence how we see them. Choosing to see the world through the lens of Christ corrects our natural distortions and helps us see life as it truly is.

Do we choose to look at life through the lens of the fruit of the Spirit—love, joy, peace, patience, kindness, goodness, faithfulness, gentleness, and self-control? As we rely on the Holy Spirit to strengthen and encourage us to live out each attribute consistently, we will find our attitudes and behaviors aligning more with Christ. A good reminder is: "Where focus goes, energy flows."

In much the same way an optometrist offers us a lens to improve our eyesight, God offers us a lens which can improve our spiritual vision. The vision we need to view life correctly is through the lens of faith.

What visions are you focusing on through the lens of Christ?

The Bible

Put on the salvation as your helmet, and take the sword of the spirit, which is the word of God. Ephesians 6:17

The Bible is the best-selling book of all time—over 20 million copies are sold annually in the United States alone. It both challenges and comforts us.

In guest Pastor Bruce Frank's sermon, he encouraged us to read the Bible. He recommended to start by reading a Psalm a day, then think about it, pray about it, and apply it. Choose to read God's Word not as a check mark or to-do list, but instead as a means to know Jesus better by leaning into His love, grace, and mercy. The Bible challenges us, yet also gives us promises to hold on to and it comforts us in times of need. In keeping God's Word there is a great reward. His Word gives us guidance to safely reach our final heavenly destination.

The Bible is God's divine road map for us. Through it the Lord shows us obstacles to avoid, warning us against wrong turns, detours, and dead ends. There's beauty in allowing Scripture to seep into our heart and convert and restore our soul. God's Word will help us make wise choices. It is both a map and a mirror. Maps guide us as we study Scripture, showing us the best route to follow along our journey. Just as a mirror reflects what we look like on the outside, His teachings reflect what we're like on the inside. In developing devotional time, there is great reward.

Reflect on God's Word by reading, reviewing, remembering, and then applying.

Treasure

You will seek me and find me, when you seek me with all your heart. Jeremiah 29:13

A Methodist minister and dear friend, Reverend Harry Baas, shared a portion of his sermon with me. He told me the story of Nicole Hadley. She was one of the victims of the massacre as students prayed around the flagpole in Paducah, Kentucky. After the tragedy, Nicole's mother told the doctors she wanted all her daughter's organs donated. It had come into conversation between mother and daughter only weeks prior to the awful event. Her mom wanted to honor Nicole's wishes. As it turned out, a retired Methodist minister received Nicole's heart. Her mom visited him in the hospital. When she entered his room, he thanked her profusely for extending his life and asked if there was anything he could do to comfort her. She asked if she could lay her head on his chest so she could hear her daughter's heartbeat one more time. My pastor friend reminded me that this is what God wants from us: to put His head on our chest and hear His Son's heartbeat.

In the Bible, David was known to be a man who had God's will and glory at heart. David's public display of worship was a fruit of his private devotions. By loving others, sharing the Gospel, praying, reading God's Word, and worshiping, our hearts become more like God's. When we pursue God's heart, even difficulties become easier because we are focusing and walking with Him. We may not face the same kind of giant David did or be called to rule a nation, but we can choose to seek God's heart.

What does your heart hold?

Cheerfulness

A cheerful heart is good medicine, but a crushed spirit dries up the bones. Proverbs 17:22 (NIV)

Solomon assures us a cheerful heart is good medicine for the mind, body, and soul. To be cheerful is to be ready to greet others with a warm welcome, a word of encouragement, enthusiasm for the task at hand, and a positive outlook for the future. When cheerful people greet us, they are as welcome as pain-relieving medicine. The connection between our physical and emotional health is undeniable. Keeping a positive, joyful spirit is a blessing to our bodies.

What a blessing it was for me to meet Ellie, a sharp-minded 101-year-old amazing woman. She was a resident at HarborChase assisted living and a special friend. Though bedridden, she radiated God's love to anyone who came into her room. She always looked put together and told me having her nails painted and hair done gave her a happy heart. Ellie said, "I'm choosing to release joy even though I'm stuck here physically. I love to look out the window at God's creation smiling at me." She quoted: "A smile is a curve that sets everything straight. Keep smiling." Though now she has gone to Heaven, she exuded joy about life and shared her opinion and wisdom freely.

It's true that authentic cheerfulness may show up on our faces when we smile, but it originates in our hearts. It's a fountain of God's love which flows onto others. Ellie's positive attitude sure overflowed onto me. She is a beautiful reminder that a cheerful heart is the best medicine.

Do you know of someone in need of the good medicine a cheerful heart brings? Why not deliver it?

Sacred Places

Now my eyes will be open and my ears attentive to the prayer offered in this place. 2 Chronicles 7:15 (NIV)

Sacred places are important in our spiritual lives. We see this throughout the Bible. They are shelters for God's people, where we are nourished and fed, and then called to go out into the world sharing God's love and presence.

Visiting an Evensong choral prayer service in London, I was captivated by how the cathedral's very magnificence testifies to the majesty of God. Looking at the stained-glass windows with the sun shining through, I could feel God's presence as the choir sang in angelic voices. We have all heard the phrase, "The church is not a building but the Body of Christ, a community of the faithful who come together to worship." Though this cathedral was breathtaking and the singing inspiring, I'm so grateful for my own church family at The Church of Eleven22. It's a place where community gathers for prayer and worship and shines with the radiance of Christ's presence. It's like the city on a hill where all are welcome to come meet with the Lord for love and redemption.

I believe it's also important to have a sacred place at home. For me, it's sitting on my back porch and lighting a candle. Spending time in God's Word, surrounded by nature, is so calming and precious. Any quiet area can be reserved to engage in devotion and prayer. It becomes a sacred space. The more we engage in these spaces, the deeper our life and its connection to God becomes.

Where is your sacred place?

Mentor

Teaching them to observe everything I have commanded you. And remember, I am with you always, to the end of the age. Matthew 28:20

After being encouraged in a sermon by Pastor Joby Martin to "seek out someone who has made a positive difference in your life," I went on a search to find Juanita Gresham. She was my seventh-grade teacher and wise mentor. It had been forty-two years since our last encounter. I was able to find her and, over lunch, tell her of the positive effect she had on my life. Juanita cried as I disclosed what an inspiration and blessing she was to me at such a young age.

I did not make the cheerleading squad and was devastated. The next day she called me into her office and said God had a plan for me. It was to start and lead a dance/pep squad at our school. With Juanita by my side, that's what we did. I told her how she had turned something so negative into something so positive.

Juanita went on to get her PhD and, at seventy-two years of age, has touched many lives as a teacher, role model, administrator, and friend. After our visit and deep conversation, it came as no surprise to learn she is a strong woman of God, and her advice and guidance to me at such a young age was laced with holy truth. As I left lunch I realized she had been divinely designated in my life, and what a blessing for me to be able to open my grateful heart to her.

I challenge you to seek out someone who has benefited your life, and share with them your grateful heart for making a difference.

Light

In the same way, let your light shine before others, so that they may see your good works and give glory to your Father who is in heaven. Matthew 5:16

I was having coffee with my friend Louise, who works in international development. Her project now is working with the UK government and Ukrainian ministries in emergency response and reconstruction programs. Her bold, helpful spirit was inspiring as she told me about her trips to Ukraine and the amazing women she encountered while in a bomb shelter during a missile strike in Lviv.

Without phone or power, one beautiful lady set up a coffee shop featuring homemade chocolates to create some kind of normality in the midst of chaos. She said it's her gift to share warmth and comfort to her fellow Ukrainians. Another woman in the shelter was once a well-known fashion designer; she now humbly and willingly sews uniforms for the military. Though their lives resemble a cold, dark winter's day, they have decided they want to be an example of salt (Matthew 5:13) and light, giving hope and inspiration to others. Their faith makes them resilient and more able to face even the most horrific conditions.

Perseverance and bravery are two key words I thought of as Louise shared the stories. Though many of us have never been in the throes of a war, we all at one time or another have faced pressures and tension, when we think we will just give up. Instead, choose to be salt and light, and pray for bridges of love and hope to be built which will transcend any war or personal conflict.

Where can you shine God's light in the darkness?

Patience

Rejoice in hope, be patient in tribulation, be constant in prayer. Romans 12:12

Frustration is defined as "an emotional response to opposition to the fulfillment of an individual's will." All of us must deal with the problem of frustration. Thomas Edison struggled to produce incandescent light. He created 523 light bulbs that didn't work. When someone asked him to think of all the time he had wasted, his response was, "I found 523 ways it couldn't be done." He had shifted his perspective of frustration into a positive.

While I was substitute teaching for kindergarten, a sweet little girl came to me with her shoes tied in many knots. She said, "There's no hope. I can't get the knots out, and I'll never learn to tie my shoes!" I told her I had the same problem when I was her age. My patient kindergarten teacher, Miss Mink, showed me how to make bunny ears as loops. As my student tried this method, she pulled her shoelaces into a bow and, with a big smile, skipped away.

Think about all the "knots," or perhaps, "nots" in our lives. Not getting what we want, not closing a deal, not getting a job, can create a feeling of frustration. This only leads to more tension—similar to yanking on shoelaces that tighten the knot. Untangling knots takes patience. If we shift our perspective, every bow on a shoe and every bow on a gift is created by going through a knot.

We all have "nots" in our lives, but instead of tugging, let's allow God to help us with patience. In our trusting Him, He reveals how, through prayer, the result can loop into a bow.

What knots can you turn into bows?

Small Deposits

He that is faithful in that which is least is faithful also in much; and he that is unjust in the least is unjust also in much.
Luke 16:10 (KJV)

Jesus reminds us frequently that how we deal with the smaller things in our day reveals if we can be trusted with bigger things. In the Bible we find many stories of lifelong repercussions which resulted from a single decision, such as Adam eating the forbidden fruit, which cost him paradise. The Bible also tells of a selfless little boy who gave Jesus his meager lunch and fed 5,000 people.

I have a glass jar filled with little things I treasure from special people: notes, cards, things made by my children, and handwritten letters from cherished loved ones. The items may seem simple, but how important they are to me! Since the passing of my parents, my reading their lovely handwritten notes brings such comfort.

Much in the same way, our life is like a jar of little things. God delights in giving us opportunities to apply and grow our faith, and often uses little things to test our integrity. Little compromises can result in big problems, and small kindnesses can result in big blessings. The little things we do in private do matter. A brief prayer for someone in need, a small act of goodwill, a handwritten note—even how we handle interruptions, difficult people, and hassles—all can have a great consequence on our lives. The little things build character as well. God does see the small, kind gestures done with no hidden agenda or personal gain.

What one small deposit can you place in someone's jar today?

Encounters

Do not neglect to show hospitality to strangers, for thereby some have entertained angels unaware. Hebrews 13:2

Visiting my parents' gravesites at Oaklawn Cemetery, I was feeling a yearning to be close to them. The Scripture above describes what happened next. I met Mr. Henry. He walks the grounds for exercise and to be close to nature, and he was on my path. When he saw me, with sincere hospitality he spoke softly to me. His outward appearance was as if he had stepped out of the Bible. He is a strong man with a deep, calm voice, gentle eyes framed by round glasses, and he has a wonderful smile. I'm unable to explain the mysterious and glorious encounter. While looking into his eyes, I felt he wasn't just any man, but as though the Lord sent Mr. Henry at this very moment to comfort me as I sat in stillness missing my parents.

We interact with other people every day: coworkers, family members, friends, plus many people we meet briefly in airports, on trains, behind counters, and in passing. How much real contact occurs is, in large measure, up to us. There is no such thing as finding Christ while avoiding others. Hospitality to strangers links us with God and with others, and it's a wonderful way of experiencing the presence of God. Oftentimes it reveals appropriate awareness of our own family history.

As I sat and spoke with Mr. Henry, I realized that my parents were part of this encounter. They had encouraged hospitality in our home and hospitality in our hearts. I'm so grateful for a divine encounter with Mr. Henry.

How can you show hospitality everywhere you go?

Compassion

Carry each other's burdens, and in this way, you will fulfill the law of Christ. Galatians 6:2 (NIV)

In Latin, *compati* means "suffer with." Compassion is an attribute by which someone sees the suffering of another and experiences true empathy for them. Someone else's heartbreak becomes your heartbreak.

My son Trey was born twenty-nine years ago and, soon after, became ill. After years of struggling to uncover what was driving my precious baby's illness, we spent weeks at Johns Hopkins in Baltimore, and at Mount Sinai in New York for answers. They figured out his illness was driven by food—he was born with life-threatening food allergies. For the first five years of his life, he could only eat nine foods and to this day he has never had birthday cake or cheese pizza.

He called me recently to share his latest allergy tests. The results showed only slight changes; he's still severely allergic to peanuts, milk, eggs, and any type of shellfish. His EpiPen continues to be a necessity and Benadryl is always on hand.

My heart was flooded with emotions as I came across his college entrance essay written more than ten years ago. He wrote how having such severe allergies has helped him to be more compassionate toward others suffering with any type of illness.

Trey turned something negative into something positive—a caring, compassionate heart rather than bitterness. He has never asked, "Why me?" saying God made him just the way He intended, and Trey uses his special needs to inspire others ... especially me.

How can you use your struggles to show compassion to others?

Transition

"For I know the plans I have for you," declares the Lord, "plans for welfare and not for evil, to give you a future and a hope." Jeremiah 29:11

Transition is defined as "the act of passing from one state or place to the next" and "an event that results in a transformation." After attending an Elevation Worship evening concert with my daughter, I reflected on the transformation God has been directing in my life. Pastor Steven Furtick had reminded us that in our lives a gate can be a symbol of transition. What we cling to will determine whether we go forward or get stuck at the gate. We are the most vulnerable entering in or coming out of a transitional period. We can't take hold of what's new if we have a death grip on something old.

Transition does not allow us to stay in the same place. Don't get trapped at the gate. Choose transformation through every change, trusting God will see us through every transition. We must keep moving forward because sometimes a miracle is in the transition.

The last few years have taught me change is necessary for growth. Our times of transition help prepare us for the change. They grow our faith and trust in God's plan for our life. Whether we experience transition under our feet, in our heart, or both, the Lord is using it for us, not against us. We can trust change is not a life hindrance; it is a life occurrence acting as a steppingstone toward God's best for us.

Don't give up during a time of transition. Hold strong to your faith and trust God to see us through. When things all around us are changing, remember God never changes.

Wisdom

Listen to advice and accept instruction, that you may gain wisdom in the future. Proverbs 19:20

While taking a walk in the woods, I was startled by seeing a large barn owl in a tree very close. It watched us and looked so wise. Ironically, I had just listened to a sermon on wisdom. In the Bible, owls are often seen as spiritual symbols representing wisdom and knowledge, and also representing divine understanding and spiritual insight. The acronym for WISE is: wisdom, inspiration, support, encouragement.

The book of Proverbs is full of wisdom. One way to gain wisdom is from the knowledge of the men and women who preceded us. Having mentors and accountability partners is important. Moses and Joshua lived out this concept. Moses was leading, and Joshua was there studying, learning, and preparing for the day leadership would change hands. After forty years of wandering and setbacks, God's people were poised to enter the Promised Land. Moses, their great leader, had died, and Joshua, his assistant, was in charge. God told Joshua to be strong and courageous. God's words of direction through Moses were to be the backbone of Joshua's leadership in every situation.

The Lord's promise to Joshua applies to us as well: *Be strong and of good courage; do not be afraid, nor be dismayed, for the Lord your God is with you wherever you go. (Joshua 1:9)* What comfort we have knowing God is with us and He places positive and wise mentors in our lives!

Who are the wise mentors leading you?

Winter

Trust

Three times a day he got on his knees, prayed and gave thanks to God, just as he had done before. Daniel 6:10

While visiting Dr. Charles Stanley's church in Atlanta, I stood captivated by a portrait of Daniel in the lions' den. The lions were circling Daniel, and there were bones scattered on the ground, but Daniel was not looking at the lions. He was standing with his hands behind him, looking up and out at a ray of light.

The name *Daniel* comes from Hebrew, meaning, "God is my judge"—an appropriate definition for one who chooses to praise God rather than please man. It was Daniel's custom to pray three times a day. Even though King Darius declared himself the only "deity" the people should pray to, Daniel continued to commit himself to God. His walk in life reflected that his faith was not simply to serve as a guide, but, more importantly, as an anchor.

Even though his commitment landed him in the lions' den, he was not altered by his circumstances. He continued to pray and praise God. After a night alone in the lions' den, Daniel emerged, unharmed, telling the king, *My god sent an angel, and shut the lions' mouths, and they have not harmed me, because I was found blameless before him. (Daniel 6:22)*

God doesn't promise us a trouble-free life, but He does promise to be with us through it all. Take time today and pray and talk to God about the lions in your life. He will give you faith and wisdom to make it through any circumstance or situation unharmed.

What or who is in your lions' den?

Disaster

My grace is sufficient for you, for my power is made perfect in weakness. 2 Corinthians 12:9

While traveling, at the airport I had an interesting encounter and great conversation with members of the popular rock band Molly Hatchet. One band member told me his favorite song to perform is "Flirtin' with Disaster." He also said he spent many years living this way, until one day he woke up and decided, in sober judgment, that if he continued flirting with disaster he would blow up his life. This famous personality now starts his day in devotion and gratefulness to God, with healthy boundaries in place. I was inspired by this rock and roll star's willingness to share how the Lord took his weakness and turned it into grace, and made him bold enough to sing the song without living a life of destruction, while humble enough to tell others of his testimony.

In our daily lives we know flirting with sin—what Pastor Joby Martin refers to as lust of the flesh, lust of the eyes, and pride of life—will lead us down the wrong path. It's vital for us to evaluate the importance of establishing safeguards in our lives. Though we're all lured by different types of sin, establishing healthy boundaries through the power of Christ helps us avoid the allurement to the enemy's sneaky, flashy bait. We know a hook is always there waiting for us to bite.

God hasn't promised that we won't suffer in this life, but He has told us He will walk through our valleys with us. How comforting it is to know He'll be right by our side and His grace will be sufficient.

When have you felt God's grace during a time of weakness?

Trials

Beloved, do not be surprised at the fiery trial when it comes upon you to test you, as though something strange were happening to you. But rejoice in so far as you share Christ's sufferings, that you may also rejoice and be glad when his glory is revealed. 1 Peter 4:12-13

When I was attending "Come Home to Hope" in New York, Pastor Joel Osteen spoke of fiery trials. No one wants to be thrown into the fire. We've all experienced these trials and though we can't avoid them, we can take great comfort that God is always right beside us, in and through them.

Joel referenced the mighty sequoia tree. Not only is it designed to withstand most forest fires, it actually needs fires in order to thrive. The sequoia needs fire for the small cone to open up and the seeds to germinate. During the fiery process, the sequoia itself is protected. The thick, spongy bark can be up to two feet thick, insulating it from fire damage. Fire is a purifying process even in forests. What looks like a trial for the sequoia is in reality the process the trees need for growth and to flourish.

The same holds true for us. During the time of our suffering we don't see the end result, but by faith we can count it as joy because we trust God. Trials will come and the heat may be intense, yet what comfort we have in His grace! He will never leave us alone.

What about you? When difficulties come into your life, do you grumble, complain, and resist, or do you respond with a humble attitude and submissive heart?

Resilience

And we know that for those who love God, all things work together for good, for those who are called according to his purpose. Romans 8:28

Like a roller coaster designed with hills and dives and sudden twists and turns, the same goes for our lives. My son, Trey, convinced me to ride the Tennessee Tornado roller coaster at Dollywood amusement park. This ride reminded me that much of life can feel like a roller coaster. Sometimes we doubt if we have the resilience to finish the bumpy and stressful ride. We dread what twists and turns are around the corner and pray we won't end up upside down.

In the Bible, we can look at the life of Moses. In the book of Exodus, we see he is an important figure with rebound power and resilience. Moses was born into slavery in Egypt and rose in importance with the ruling family. After killing an Egyptian, he fled. Eventually, Moses met an angel from God in a burning bush. Moses led the Israelites away from Egypt after bringing plagues to that country, as directed by God.

Although he experienced several traumatic events, Moses never surrendered to the ordeals of his life. He continued with the mission given to him by God, trusting Him even in paralyzing circumstances.

We don't have to wait for a traumatic event to develop a resilient personality. In the Bible you will find the phrase "it came to pass" 465 times. Storms in life will certainly come, yet having an eternal focus keeps peace within our soul, no matter how bumpy the ride.

Where has God shown you resilience and hope to withstand and learn from difficult experiences?

Angels

Suddenly, the angel was joined by a vast host of others—the armies of heaven—praising God and saying, "Glory to God in highest heaven, and peace on earth to those with whom God is pleased." Luke 2:13-14

Scripture gives us a lovely picture of praise in the above verse. When Jesus was born, Gabriel, an angel of the Lord, appeared to the shepherds and shared the good news. Then many other angels joined together to praise God.

Angels serve as role models of worship. The word *angel* literally means "messenger." In Luke 1:30-31, *And the Angel said to her, "Do not be afraid, Mary, for you have found favor with God. And behold, you will conceive in your womb and bear a son, and you shall call his name Jesus."* Through worship, angels spread the news of God's glory and exhibit holy reference.

Keeping Christ at the center of Christmas is an intentional act of worship. It requires a heart of adoration much like the angels have. When Jesus is the focus of our holiday, we are centered on His love, peace, and joy.

My very special friend, Stephanie, gave me a beautiful book: *Anne Neilson's Angels: Devotions and Art to Encourage, Refresh, and Inspire*, which I keep on my coffee table. I opened it again this morning and read how the author-artist signed my book: "May there always be an angel in your midst."

Especially during the Christmas season, think about the angels in your midst and the messages they deliver.

Shelter

He who dwells in the shelter of the Most High will abide in the shadow of the Almighty. Psalm 91:1

I have been reading and studying Psalm 91, and printed it as a covenant prayer to pray over myself and my loved ones. We can take refuge in the presence of the Lord, knowing that nothing can separate us from God's love. That is what Psalm 91 is all about—shelter. Our Heavenly Father has a secret place in His arms which protects us from the storms raging in the world around us. To abide in the shadow of the Almighty, we must first choose to dwell in the shelter of the Most High. When life is draining us and there seems to be no time or place to rest, this Psalm is comforting and reassuring. Understanding this enables us to be at peace, no matter our present circumstances.

Most of us have experienced difficult times when there seemed to be no easy way out. Our first reaction might be to try to escape as quickly as possible, ignore it, or solve the mess on our own. However, I've learned that my soul's deepest need is not the removal of my sufferings, but for the presence of God in the midst of suffering and trusting His guidance. He knows the darkness of the painful place, and He's the one Who will lead us out of the darkness and bring us into the light. What comfort that He provides shelter, and we can abide in the shadow of the Almighty! Don't be afraid of shadows. It means there's light nearby.

Where do you seek shelter?

Spread Joy

Light in a messenger's eyes brings joy to the heart, and good news gives health to the bones. Proverbs 15:30 (NIV)

While at Mayo Clinic hospital waiting for my dad to come out of surgery, I met Alicia and her therapy dog, Lil' Bit. Alicia comes weekly to share her sweet dog with patients and their loved ones. Lil' Bit's tender and sweet nature calmed the entire waiting room, surrounded us with joy, and relieved our anxiety. She brought a message of God's love and understanding. Then Alicia told us God wants us to take the blessings we have received and pass them along to others we encounter, especially those in need.

Many a grieving heart is comforted by a pet whose love and loyalty makes pain and loss more bearable. According to Harvard Medical School, a dog can actually lower blood pressure and cholesterol, and reduce anxiety. It's also proven there is only a thin separation between one's emotional health and physical health.

Alicia uses Lil' Bit's story to bless others. The dog was rescued after Hurricane Irma hit in 2017. Abandoned, wounded, and wandering in flooded waters, the dog was found by Alicia's daughter, who trained her to become a service dog and was her constant companion until she sadly passed away. Alicia, grieving from her daughter's passing, decided to train Lit' Bit as a therapy dog to bless others. Through it all, Lil' Bit has also helped Alicia heal her grieving heart.

Listening to her story, I watched Lil' Bit move around the waiting room, bringing light and joy. She warmed my heart. I'm grateful that Lil' Bit—a true survivor of Hurricane Irma—took the time to sprinkle kindness and calm others.

Rushing

Be still and know that I am God. Psalm 46:10

Pastor Joby Martin gave a sermon at church in which he spoke of this Scripture and how it reminds us to slow down. Stop rushing to be everywhere, everyone, and everything "because what is impossible with man is possible with God." Pastor Joby also reflects on this in his books, *If the Tomb Is Empty: Why the Resurrection Means Anything Is Possible* and *Anything Is Possible: How Nine Miracles of Jesus Reveal God's Love for You.*

Often, the pace of our lives mimics the pace of our hearts. We don't take the opportunity to "be still, and know."

God is at work in the waiting. Abraham was promised an heir through his wife Sarah despite her age. This period of waiting lasted twenty-five years. Sarah did eventually give birth to Isaac *and the Lord did to Sarah as he had promised. (Genesis 21:1)* God has a purpose and a plan in times of waiting. He can see things which may need to be ironed out in our hearts, that would remain creased if it weren't for the refining times of waiting patiently.

I reflected on this as we shared a delicious lunch and great fellowship with special friends. Before our lovely afternoon together ended, we joined hands and prayed. What comfort it is that we can drop our worries at His feet and rest in His unchanging character of love and peace. When we do so we feel refreshed, refueled, and ready to continue our day at a slower and calmer pace.

In the midst of our busy and hectic full days, let's stop for a few minutes, focus on what is most important, and ask God to make our hearts more like His.

Disappointment

Though the fig tree bears no fruit and there are no grapes on the vines, though the olive crop fails, and the fields produce no food, so there are no sheep in the pen, and no cattle in the stalls, but I will rejoice in the Lord, I will be joyful in God my Savior. Habakkuk 3:17-18 (NIV)

Many things in life may disappoint us. Disappointment is a powerful force. It's the first seed of doubt that intrudes our faith, and often leads to discouragement which robs us of peace, joy, and contentment.

Disappointment sounds so harmless, but it is the beginning of a wedge which will stunt our spiritual growth. When we place our expectations on people, situations, or circumstances, we are usually disappointed at some point. However, when we choose to look to God for guidance during our feelings of disappointment, we can then be reappointed … trusting Him to move us forward, shifting our focus toward Him.

God made us with an empty space in our innermost being that only He can fill. Disappointment is temporary, and in His time God will restore us. Through the process He will make us strong, firm, and steadfast for our growth in His glory. Endurance is the decision or determination to focus on the goodness and character of God when disappointment creeps in. *Character* is a word which refers to the test of precious metal when it's refined in the fire and comes through this testing purified. When disappointment tries to invade us during difficult seasons, let's cast our cares on God!

In what areas of your life do you need to turn to God to shift from your disappointment to reappointment?

True Faith

For all things are for your sakes, that the abundant grace might through the thanksgiving of many redound to the glory of God. For which cause we faint not; but though our outward man perish, yet the inward man is renewed day by day. 2 Corinthians 4:15-16 (KJV)

What directs our decisions, actions, words, and thoughts? Unlike blind faith, true faith isn't dependent on what we think, feel, or believe at any given moment. True faithfulness relies on God. Circumstances may go from bad to worse; however, true faith not only perseveres through testing, it also makes us stronger during the process when we choose to lean on God and His promises.

This made me think of my special friend Eddie Wright, who recently passed away. He was fighting pancreatic cancer yet continued preaching and praising God as a visiting pastor to churches. What a privilege it was to see him live out his faith as a witness to others while preaching at He Changed My Mind Ministries in Callahan, Florida. Eddie spoke of not just getting his body right; he worked on getting his heart right to be pleasing to God because the inward man—both physical and spiritual—is renewed day by day when we live in faith. With true faith, we can walk confidently into the future, knowing that God is able to hold us, sustain us, empower us, heal us, and strengthen us no matter what is thrown our way.

The more we apply God's promises to our everyday battles, the more our faith will be strengthened. By faith, we can trust that the same God Who controls the wind and the waves also controls the circumstances in our lives.

Eddie called it "Take it and turn it." What can you take and turn?

No Complaining

Do all things without grumbling or disputing. Philippians 2:14

Today I encourage you to adopt a "no complaining rule" and go on a complaining fast. Not because it will make everyone around you happier—although it will—but because it will help you experience more of the peace and joy God wants for you, and it will help you build strong, positive relationships with others.

While substituting at school this week, I had a student who complained about everything. He didn't like his assigned seat. He hated art. The room was too hot, and so on. I noticed no one wanted to be around him, and by the end of class neither did I. However, I did take the time to talk to him about his attitude. To my surprise, he said he didn't even realize it. The popular book by Will Bowen, *A Complaint Free World: How to Stop Complaining and Start Enjoying the Life You Always Wanted*, sold 30 million copies. It challenged people to go twenty-one days without complaining. Those who responded to the challenge said they felt much better as a result.

Complaining is a habit that not only sabotages our happiness, it degrades the morale of our family and friends. We have the power to choose our beliefs and actions. And when we focus on the positive instead of the negative, we'll find the faith, strength, and confidence to take on life's challenges. Remember, the people we most enjoy being around are positive in their conversation. They believe the best about anyone and are not eager to find fault.

When you got up this morning, what did you say: "Good morning, Lord," or "Oh Lord, is it already morning!" It is our choice.

Integrity

Whoever walks in integrity walks securely, but he who makes his ways crooked will be found out. Proverbs 10:9

Pastor Andy Stanley preached an enlightening sermon on integrity. I was surprised to learn that the word *integrity* is in the top ten most looked-up words in the Merriam-Webster online dictionary. The definition of integrity is: "the quality of being honest and having strong moral principals; uprightness."

In math, an integer is a whole number. In society, a person with integrity is someone not divided. As Christ's followers we're committed to living by God's standards, such as maintaining our integrity—saying what we mean and doing what we say. Having integrity means we are the same in the open as we are behind closed doors. Andy reminded us that integrity means being honest and whole and keeping our word. He challenged us in his sermon to ask ourselves: Do I say I will do things, and they don't get done? Do I make excuses for not following through? When under pressure, is my trigger response to cover, hide, avoid, or tell half-truths?

Integrity will define the health and depth of our relationships. A lack of integrity will always keep us and others off-balance. Since we all make mistakes, Andy reinforced that when we mess up, we must show up, own up, and then clean up. The health of all our relationships and respect is contingent on our integrity, not our infallibility. Integrity is the glue holding our way of life together. No integrity = no trust.

Do your choices reflect integrity?

Hope

Rejoice in hope, be patient in tribulation, be constant in prayer. Romans 12:12

Think of all the things your hands have done. We often use our hands to push things out of our way, to protect ourselves, or to strike back. When we drop our hands it can make us feel defenseless and vulnerable. In the face of all life's difficult circumstances, we can surrender our hearts and raise our hands in prayer, knowing and trusting God's hands are busy on our behalf.

In an interview, Rick Warren, the author of *The Purpose Driven Life*, and his wife, Kay, shared that five days after the thirty-third birthday of his Saddleback Church, their youngest son, Matthew, committed suicide after years of struggling with mental illness. Rick said, "There is purpose even in our pain." His wife said she is devastated but not destroyed, and it's important for people to know that no matter how desperate their despair, there is always hope. Kay created a hope box filled with Scriptures as a reminder: God is our refuge and strength and is present to help in our troubles. She reads from her hope box each morning, knowing with God by her side there is always hope. Their strength and trust in God through their devastating loss and grief is a true testament of their faith.

I find comfort knowing God holds me in His hands and gives me hope when I need it. Faith is strengthened by leaving everything in God's hands and trusting His hand in all things.

What do you need to let go of and place in the loving hands of God?

Attitude

Finally, brothers, whatever is true, whatever is honorable, whatever is just, whatever is pure, whatever is lovely, whatever is commendable, if there is anything worthy of praise, think about these things. Philippians 4:8

I promised my mother before she passed away I would continue to visit her friends and caregivers in her memory care unit at HarborChase. While at an open house, I had an opportunity to visit her friends and thank my mom's caregivers. These fine ladies were smiling and full of the Holy Spirit as I watched them tenderly care for the residents. I left with a heart overflowing with gratitude for their positive attitude while doing a difficult job.

More than skill, knowledge, or aptitude, our attitude plays a huge role in our life. A healthy, positive attitude comes from within our heart, mind, body, and spirit. It can't be bought or manufactured. We can't inject it, swallow it, or transfer it because we already possess it. It begins with a decision—one we make. We sometimes wrongly believe attitude is something we are born with, rather than a choice we make. It's also important that we show others our gratitude for choosing a positive attitude, especially when they are doing what appears to be an extremely difficult job.

When we are grateful for what God is doing in our life and we express it, we attract more to be grateful for, and if we complain, we will have more to complain about. An attitude of gratitude is the highest expression of faith. A negative attitude could hurt us, yet choosing a positive attitude never will, so why not go with the positive.

What attitude will you choose today?

Battles

Oh come, let us worship and bow down; let us kneel before the Lord, our Maker! Psalm 95:6

W hile sitting outside as a storm approached, I watched the gusts of wind create wild swirling movements in the branches of a large oak tree in my yard. After listening to a sermon on "Bend but don't break," I realized that, like the oak tree, we are created to do just that—remain strong in our connection to the Lord, yet also have enough flexibility to be able to sway back and forth when challenging times come our way. We can withstand so much more than we think is possible when our roots are deep in Christ and we place our trust in Him.

We've all experienced periods in our lives when a particular problem, person, or situation keeps us up at night. I discovered when that happens, getting down on my knees and asking God to please help me stay focused on Him, He comforts me. Thinking about the Lord brings peace. The larger our thoughts about God, the smaller our thoughts about whatever problem we're facing. We can lean on Him and His abundant provision, protection, and love, and release the people or circumstances trying to heap hatred or destruction upon us hoping to discourage and break us. As we invite God in, He substitutes peace for pressure, and a positive mindset replaces a negative one. The Hebrew word for "kneeling in prayer" can be translated to mean "bow down" or "worship." Dr. Charles Stanley said, "Fight all your battles on your knees and you win every time."

When storms are swirling and the winds of adversity blow, do you seek the Lord?

Stillness

Be still and know that I am God. Psalm 46:10

In our fast-paced culture it's not easy to be still. Our society is overstimulated and overcommitted. This can create anxiety, causing us to lose peace and become overwhelmed. The Hebrew word for *still* is *Raphah*, which means "to sink down, relax, let go of." Often, this is the last thing we feel like doing when our world is spinning out of control. We can find comfort and rest as we ruminate on this Scripture, knowing that even when troubles threaten to overtake us, God's presence surrounds us.

We do so much rushing, often we forget to simply be still and listen for God to speak. Finding quiet time is an essential part of each day—a time to read the Bible, pray, and just be still. No matter how chaotic the world may become around us, we can find quietness and strength in our Heavenly Father's love and presence. Spending quiet time in nature, surrounded by His creation, is a way He speaks to me. Today, take a moment to breathe and, in stillness, relax into a posture of resting with Him. Spending time in the presence of the Holy Spirit brings peace and draws us closer to God's nearness and His love. He is our refuge and our strength.

By choosing to surrender our noisy lives and cluttered minds to God, we can learn to be still and hear His gentle whisper. What a blessing to receive His love, peace, and guidance in stillness with Him.

What do you need Jesus to calm in your mind and heart? Pause for a moment, and hear Him inviting you into the stillness of God's presence.

The Enemy

He plied him with many questions, but Jesus gave him no answer. Luke 23:9 (NIV)

Our Bible study group, led by my dear friend Angi, has been meeting for over twenty years, and I'm so grateful to be surrounded by such amazing sisters in Christ. We are reading and studying Louie Giglio's book, *Don't Give the Enemy a Seat at Your Table: It's Time to Win the Battle of Your Mind* .... In it we are reminded that we don't have to let negative thoughts or people control our life or influence our thinking. Jesus invites us to the table He has prepared for us—where the enemy is not invited. That needs to be our response when thinking about or dealing with toxic people or situations. God's answer is to not engage, participate, or respond to a hateful assault. Jesus led by example when dealing with King Herod. Instead of arguing, Jesus gave no answer, as we read in Luke 23:9.

It's interesting to ponder that negative criticisms are usually more of a reflection of the person criticizing than they are about us. The critic projects their own insecurities onto others. Critics tend to bully or intimidate so they can feel powerful.

Jesus was never manipulated or controlled. He was mission-focused and others-centered. He also demonstrated the need to walk away when dealing with a toxic person. When they don't get what they want, they tend to stir up strife. Pray for them, but don't let them steal your joy. My pastor, Joby Martin, says, "Don't get in the mud and wrestle with a pig." And don't allow the negativity of others to have a seat at your table.

Who sits at your table?

Peace

*For God is not a God of disorder but a God of peace. 1
Corinthians 14:33 (NIV)*

I have learned many beautiful things from Frances
Keiser, my publishing assistant, and now dear friend
and wise mentor. She is a naturalist, wildlife rescue
volunteer, author, publisher, and friend to animals and
children. One thing in particular she's taught me is that a
well-designed page in a book isn't just what you see. It's also
what you don't see.

This area is called white space, and it carries as much
importance as the words on the page. A page with lots of
white space invites us in. It doesn't feel crowded or chaotic;
it feels peaceful. White space gives the reader a mental
break while drawing attention to what's most important.

The same is true in our lives. If our lives are
overcrowded and cluttered, we feel chaotic and drained.
Feeling exhausted, overwhelmed, and overworked will only
lead us to discouragement. We need to build margins in our
lives, with some white space spent in stillness and peaceful
rest in God's presence. Spending quiet time with Him will
help us make better decisions and create healthy boundaries
so we are able to love Him and others well.

There are many examples of Jesus going off in solitude
and silence to pray and listen to God. Seeking open spaces
was something Moses lived out as he led a nation of stubborn
and rebellious people. He often withdrew to rest and find
guidance in peace—the white space of God's presence.

Where do you seek the white space of God's peace in
your life?

Aging

He who began a good work in you will bring it to completion at the day of Jesus Christ. Philippians 1:6

Sometimes we find blessings in the most difficult situations. It was difficult to walk through the doors of Grand Living at Tamaya. My dad spent his final months here. He made many wonderful friends whom I had the privilege to know and love too. The wounds of his passing made it painful, yet I knew he would love me to visit them.

So I did. Oh, what a beautiful night. While having dinner with my dad's friends, I was fascinated by the table conversation. The ladies referred to themselves as the busy bees. They are precious, kind, and live life to the fullest every day, even in their mid- to late-eighties.

"What's your secret?" I asked. Barbara said many elderly choose coping and coasting instead of blooming and thriving. She wears bright-colored clothing with matching earrings, saying that you feel good when you look good. Joyce, referred to as the "Energizer Bunny," sat across the table in a bright top covered in hearts. She herself has a big, beautiful heart and chooses happiness daily. Each day they share five things they are thankful for, saying a spirit of gratitude, more than anything else, will help determine whether you grow old gracefully—or just grow old.

The common denominator I found was each one of these women chooses to serve Christ and others. They use their talents: sewing, knitting, painting, and crafting to bring comfort for those in need all around the world. As we held hands and prayed, the warmth and comfort I felt from these special ladies was indescribable.

Advent

May the God of hope fill you with all joy and peace in believing, that you may abound in hope by the power of the Holy Spirit.
Romans 15:13

Christmastime is one of my favorite times of the year. I love all the traditions, music, decorations, and spirit of Christmas.

While growing up, we always looked forward to the customary Advent wreath on our table. We lit one of the four candles each week leading to Christmas, and the fifth, central candle, on Christmas Day. My dad explained to us the meaning and representations of the Advent season. The Advent wreath is made of evergreen, symbolizing everlasting life, and it is circular, as a never-ending symbol of eternal love and rebirth. The four candles of Advent represent the four Sundays of Advent before Christmas and they respectively symbolize hope, peace, joy, and love.

The word *advent* is derived from the Latin word *adventus*, meaning "coming." The Advent season not only symbolizes the waiting for Christ's birth, but also His final return. The Advent wreath first appeared in Germany in 1839. A Lutheran minister working at a mission for children created a wreath from the wheel of a cart and added candles, which evolved into what we see in churches today.

Though Advent is a good way to enter the season, the central focus to my love of Christmas is the wonder and the glory of Christ's entrance into the world because it gave us a reason to hope. Jesus' coming is hope fulfilled and hope assured.

As we prepare for Christmas, let's share the reason for our hope, peace, joy, and love.

Simplicity

For our boast is this, the testimony of our conscience, that we behaved in the world with simplicity and godly sincerity, not by earthly wisdom but by the grace of God, and supremely so toward you. 2 Corinthians 1:12

While I was teaching kindergarten, a precious little girl was telling us her mom made her a beautiful Christmas dress to celebrate Jesus' birthday. As I thought about our conversation, I reflected that my sweet mom also made me a beautiful Christmas dress during each of my growing-up years. We spent hours in the fabric store flipping through big pattern books. My mom's favorite was the Simplicity catalog. There was a sewing chart with each pattern. Their slogan was "Learn to sew the fun, easy way with Simplicity." My mom would say simplicity is also the best way to live.

Simplicity can be defined as "a celebration of the little things." The discipline of simplicity should be our lifestyle, reflecting simple gracious love which shines Christ's light through our lives. By seeking a simpler lifestyle and taking off the veneer of the material world, we'll discover a host of surprise gifts by walking in the footsteps of Christ. Simplicity will help us receive and enjoy the little things, and the first person who benefits from this attribute is the one who possesses it.

As we approach Christmas, let's not allow the complexity of the season or our circumstances drown out the simplicity of God's message. Hear God's call to a new way of life. Embrace the simplicity of loving and being loved as we celebrate His birth.

Merry Christmas!

Dreams

"For I know the plans I have for you," declares the Lord, "plans to prosper you and not to harm you, plans to give you hope and a future." Jeremiah 29:11 (NIV)

As we prepare to enter a new year, think about the direction our life is moving: backward or forward? On Sunday, Pastor Russ Austin delivered an inspiring message called "Bigger Dreams."

When I was a young girl, I had wonderful teachers who inspired and encouraged me. I dreamed of being a teacher too. I played school for hours in my mom's high heels, with my chalkboard. My sweet neighborhood friends were willing pupils. I was the teacher. I gave tests, graded papers, passed out treats, and supervised games. I loved playing this part. While listening to Pastor Russ's sermon, I reflected how, many years later—although I didn't pursue a teaching career—this dream became a reality for me as a substitute teacher and with other opportunities to mentor students by helping them strive for their God-given dreams.

Do you have a God-inspired dream? It's critical. Without a God-inspired dream we move listlessly through life. God will birth a dream, and the dream will drive you. Great dreamers have an inspired imagination filled with hope. Faith turns God-given dreams into reality.

To truly enjoy the abundant life Jesus came to give us, let a fresh flow of the river of God penetrate our hearts. Press into God and don't give up on your dream. To end his message, Pastor Russ prayed that our dream is fueled by the desire for God's Kingdom in our life.

What steps can you take today toward your God-given dream? Why wait?

God's Light

When Jesus spoke again to the people, he said, "I am the light of the world. Whoever follows me will never walk in darkness, but will have the light of life." John 8:12 (NIV)

While driving in the darkness, I was suddenly surrounded by dense fog. I found even my brightest headlights were only able to light up a few feet in front of the car. It caused me to slow down and clutch the steering wheel harder. I felt my heart race since I know accidents can easily happen when we can't see things clearly. The same is true in life. When we go through foggy periods, we need God's light to lead the way.

The word "light" is directly synonymous with God Himself. God led the Israelites in the desert with light through a pillar of cloud by day and a pillar of fire by night. When the pillar of light moved forward, the Israelites followed.

The Lord provides light for our souls when we look to Him. God is faithful to lead us, and He brings light and clarity through foggy times. He knows what is around the corner and on the other side of the fog, even when we can't fully see. No matter what our current situation, we can trust that God's presence will light our path, guiding and guarding us as we go along.

We must not panic because we cannot see into the future. We can't let the fear of the unknown paralyze or consume us when we are blinded by a fog. Instead, bring God's light into the darkness.

What do you do when a fog rolls in?

Heart

He gives snow like wool; he scatters frost like ashes. He hurls down his crystals of ice like crumbs; who can stand before his cold? He sends out his word, and melts them; he makes his wind blow and the waters flow. Psalm 147:16-18

What does winter mean to you? Every place on earth experiences some sort of winter season. Living in Florida, we may not have sub-zero temperatures, snow, and ice, but there is a time when temperatures drop and nature appears to pause.

This pause can remind us to pause too, take inventory of our lives, and do a heart check. How many times have we allowed our hearts to become frozen? Through unhealthy relationships, betrayal, disappointments, and unfaithfulness, our hearts can become cold and hardened. This path leads to bitterness and cynicism, closing us off to the opportunities of healthy, new, faithful relationships. We see the world and others differently and stop seeing the beauty around us.

We are reminded in John 4 to *love one another, for love is from God.* By opening up to God's love, we open our heart to love others. Even though we may feel frozen by the world around us, by accepting God's love and His will, our hearts will defrost because only God can truly melt a frozen heart. Through prayerful reflection, trusting, and patience, our hearts and the hearts of those around us will be warmed by the love of God, no matter the temperature.

After prayerful reflection, are there areas of your heart that may need defrosting by the warmth of God's love?

Winter

Therefore, if anyone is in Christ, he is a new creation; old things have passed away; behold, all things have become new. 2 Corinthians 5:17 (NKJV)

There is something refreshing about beginning a new year. It's a time to reflect on the past and move on and embrace a fresh start. It's the fresh start we can have in Christ. God's grace is designed to completely redefine our lives. The limits we have lived with can be changed and everything can be turned into a testimony of God's goodness and His power to reshape us.

Job is a good example. Job endured all kinds of problems. He lost his family, his fortune, and his health, yet he never lost his faith in Christ. Instead of becoming bitter, he kept his focus on the big picture, and God restored him, giving him a new beginning. When God gives us a new beginning, it starts with an ending. Be thankful for closed doors. They often guide us to the right one.

Lasting, redefining change first begins deep in our heart. We can experience freedom from the negative things or people that we have allowed to define us in our past, but only as we discover the power of our new identity in Christ. We can let go and move forward. Let's shake off the old and embrace all things as new as we honor God.

What do you need to release to allow for a new beginning?

Thank you for joining me on this journey through the different seasons in life. My prayer is that as you travel through, you will choose to see the blessings along the way.

With God's love,

♥ Vickie

Made in the USA
Columbia, SC
01 February 2024

30848325R00072